"Each year, salmon and steelhead return to hundreds of beautiful streams to spawn in the wild places of their birth. We should all find one such stream and try to understand it. Walk along its banks. Touch its water. Fish in it. Watch it through the seasons. And protect it."

C. BARR TAYLOR

SHADOW OF

HarperCollins*West*

A Division of HarperCollinsPublishers

A Tehabi Book

THE RAIN COAST

They say there are five stages in a fly fisherman's life. First to catch a fish on a fly, then to catch a lot of small fish, then to catch a big fish, then to catch a lot of big fish, then to catch a wild winter steelhead. I decided it was time to pursue the latter. If I catch one, I will let it go because in the Pacific Northwest many of the wild salmon and steelhead runs are perilously close to extinction.

WHERE WILD RIVERS RUN

Northwest of Juneau, along the vast snow-capped mountains that rise straight up from the deep green sea, long turquoise glaciers cut deep valleys. We fish the Situk River. Brooke, who has the bear-stopping gun, is far up the trail ahead of me, searching for a fishing hole. I walk nervously along the bear trail, head bowed to avoid the brush above, talking loudly to scare the bears and stepping on bear scat dimpled with the remains of berries and bones.

THE SALMON PEOPLE

For the Northwest Coast natives, the salmon were not mere fish but Salmon People, sending their young men and women in fish disguise to meet the human race and provide food. They happily sacrificed their flesh if the humans would help their spirits return to their magic village under the sea.

THE ILLUSTRATED SALMON

A visual celebration of the transformed salmon. Fish reentering the streams from the ocean undergo a rapid physiologic transformation. Once in the stream, they have one goal in mind—to return to the site of their origin and mate. Soon their flesh and bones nourish the stream that once gave them life.

THE SALMON

by C. Barr Taylor

ACKNOWLEDGEMENTS

I owe thanks to the following people for their generous advice and support during this project: Frank Amato, Timothy Baker, Tom Bird, Liddie Conquest, Paul Ehrlich, Jim Ferguson, John Geible, Alan Grover, Rob Jones, Alan Lufkin, Dave Narver, Andy Newman, Rich Shanteau, Miho Simonovic, Wallace Stegner, Phil Sullivan, Brooke Taylor, June Taylor, Suesan Taylor, Doug Vincent-Lang. Joy Parker freed my writing and nourished my imagination. Beth Sherman provided immeasurable assistance in the preparation and development of the manuscript. I am particularly grateful to Tom Lewis and the staff at Tehabi whose creativity, imagination, hard work, vision and support brought this book to life. — *C. Barr Taylor*

Shadow of the Salmon is the second in a series of wildlife books we have had the pleasure to conceive and produce for HarperCollins*West*. As in *Seasons of the Coyote,* our first title in this series, we have attempted to capture the spirit and fascinating plight of the wondrous creatures with which we share our world. It is our privilege in presenting the story of the salmon to share Barr Taylor's captivating text along with the beautiful images created by each of our photographers. — *Tehabi Books*

Shadow of the Salmon was developed and produced by Tehabi Books, Del Mar, CA. Joy Parker, *Editor;* Andy Lewis, *Art Director;* Sam Lewis, *Illustrator;* Nancy Cash, *Managing Editor;* Tom Lewis, *Editorial and Design Director;* Sharon Lewis, *Controller;* Chris Capen, *President.*

Library of Congress Cataloging-in-Publication Data
Taylor, C. Barr (Craig Barr), 1945-
    Shadow of the salmon: a fly fisherman's quest for the the vanishing wild salmon / C. Barr Taylor:
        p. cm.
    ISBN 0-06-258558-4 : $24.95(paperback)
    1. Pacific salmon fishing. 2. Fly fishing. I. Title,
SH686.T39 1994
333.95'6—dc20   94-26511
                                                                                          CIP

Printed in Hong Kong by Dai Nippon

PHOTO CREDITS:

Front Cover:	*R. Valentine Atkinson*	Copyright Page:	*R. Valentine Atkinson*
Back Cover:	*R. Valentine Atkinson*	Map Illustrations:	*Sam Lewis*
First Page:	*Ray Atkeson*	Salmon illustrations:	*Tom Lewis*
Table of Contents:	*Rick Shafer*	Watercolors:	*Barr Taylor*

PROLOGUE

WILD PACIFIC SALMON. THEY ASCEND great streams and surmount all obstacles to reach the tiny creek of their origin, managing to survive the million-to-one odds against them. They can lie in a foot of water and from a still start jump two feet out of the water (some say ten). In better times, during the peak of their migrations, they changed the green streams to bloodred because of their immense numbers. Their arrival and abundance causes even those great predators, the grizzly bear and the bald eagle, to shed their instinctive fear of one another and feast side-by-side on the thrashing, mating fish. Their return to the stream was celebrated as a major religious event by Pacific tribes, whose lives depended on them. These fish are great fighters, strong enough to pull a fisherman from the shore. Salmon embody one of nature's greatest miracles—the migration of species, the connection of genes to time and space. They dramatize creation, duration and destruction. Unless we act, these wild fish may become extinct in our lifetime. They are the victims of dams, pollution, overharvesting, destruction of their habitat, fish-farming, and our own bad and good intentions. We will always have salmon to eat, but we may lose the wild salmon and the wilderness that once sustained them. In the nineteenth century in California alone, they spawned in over sixty-five hundred miles of streams that stretched from the Oregon border to Southern California. Now they have access to less than five hundred miles of streams. Over sixteen million of them once entered the Columbia River, some swimming as far north as Glacier National Park on the Montana/Canada border and as far east as the Sawtooth Mountains of Idaho. Now only a few thousand return to a much-diminished territory.

When I was seven or eight, my family vacationed at Redfish Lake Lodge in the Sawtooth Mountain Range in Idaho. Back then, in the fifties, sockeye salmon still spawned in the lake after traveling over 900 miles to get there. They started their voyage at the mouth of the Columbia River, swam past Portland and then 200 more miles along the Washington/Oregon border. They turned right at Burbank, Washington, and swam another 180 miles into the Snake River in Idaho. They went up the River of No Return, so named because once you started down it, there were no roads out until you reached French Creek 80 miles down from the launch site. They have swum in these waters since the Ice Age. They swam past their namesake, Salmon, Idaho, and they kept swimming until they reached Redfish Lake. I saw those big, tired sockeye salmon, pieces of flesh dripping from their bodies, spawning along the lake shoreline. My dad said we couldn't fish there because the salmon were spawning and didn't want to be disturbed. I was disturbed that I couldn't throw a spinner with three sharp hooks in after them. In 1992 only one sockeye came up to the lake.

What has happened to these fish in the Columbia and other rivers on the Pacific Coast is a story involving mountains, rivers and oceans, and all the factors affecting them. It involves nations, vast economic interests, power, water and population. Wild salmon reflect our care of the world. Their story also involves a lot of people who care very much about these fish.

I wonder why I have become so fascinated by salmon. I like to catch them, preferably at the end of a fly line, and then to let them go—although I have caught many for supper while party-boat fishing outside the Golden Gate or kept a few for a streamside dinner. I have had great fun with these fish or, more accurately, in being in the places where the fish go. They have created an excuse for adventures with my friends and family and have taken me on an ever-widening journey of our planet. This book is about Pacific salmon and steelhead and the places I have found them. I once fished the River Traful in Argentina in ecstasy—not only because I caught a beautiful salmon, but because I did so on a stream so clear and still that I could watch the bright fly at the end of my line pass by the salmon lying on the bottom of the stream twenty feet in front of me. I stood in a valley lined by grotesque limestone outcroppings, gates to the snowcapped Chilean Andes looming in the background, on a day that felt like autumn in the Rockies. At any moment I knew a great condor might fly by. I felt at home in this rugged valley. I have had many such experiences in pursuit of Pacific Coast salmon, and the best are recounted in this book.

In my youth in Salt Lake City, salmon were remote and romantic. My father fished for them in Hell's Canyon in Idaho, flying in and landing on some remote, dubious dirt strip. I have a picture of my brother at age ten, barely able to hold up the salmon that stretches from his toes to his chin. I keep some of my father's salmon flies in a felt-lined tin. I am looking at one now: yellow and orange hackles surround the gold ribbing tied around a long, bright orange tail. I imagine him with his friends, standing in an Idaho stream and casting this fly into a deep hole. Wouldn't it be something for me to catch with this same fly the descendent of a fish my father may have caught a half century before?

Yet my father never taught my brother or me to fly-fish. We fished all over the West, mainly from a fourteen-foot fiberglass boat painted bright red that my father and his friend Vard glued together one winter for trolling the mountain reservoirs. I don't know why my father didn't bother to teach us the skills he had so obviously mastered, as had his father before him. By the time we were old enough to fish, when I was about six, he had stopped fly-fishing, preferring the comfort and ease of fishing

R. Valentine Atkinson

Many people think of Pacific Coast salmon as comprising only five species: the chinook (a.k.a. the king, tyee or spring), the coho (or silver), the chum (or dog), the pink (or humpback), and the sockeye. Recently the steelhead, which used to be considered a seagoing rainbow trout, was reclassified as a salmon. Although it returns to the sea after spawning, unlike the other five species of salmon, its structure and genetics resemble a salmon more closely than a trout.

from a boat. I know he was good with a fly rod because as a very young boy I watched him fish some beaver ponds on the upper Smith and Morehouse in the Wasatch Mountains in Utah. He would approach the side of the ponds like a cat stalking a bird, stopping far enough away so as not to spook the fish. Then he'd estimate how much line was needed to reach the fish, pull it off the reel and let it coil at his feet. After a few false casts he'd bring the whole line into the air. Then he'd set the fly forward, letting it drop gently onto the water, much like the blue-wing olive mayflies it was meant to imitate—right in front of the little brown trout that eagerly grabbed it. My father died when I was in my late twenties before I had gained my passion for the sport, and I regret that I never fly-fished with him.

In the seventies I used to drive to Yellowstone and Montana by myself in the fall. I never caught many fish, but I loved to be on the waters when the crowds had gone. When I started fishing with my brother, who actually knew how to fly-fish, he taught me there was more to the sport than simply being in nice places and flailing away. You could catch fish. The last week in June became a ritual for us: we traveled to Henry's Fork in northeastern Idaho to greet the fabled green drake mayfly hatch. We abandoned our good eating habits and ate stacks of honey scones drenched in butter at the Chalet Restaurant where we sat next to the familiar faces of those who came, as we did, year after year for this event. A few years ago most of the fish died off during the winter because too little water was released from the Island Park Reservoir a few miles above this stretch of the stream. This tragedy taught me that we must never take the life of our rivers for granted. They say that the fishing at Henry's Fork is coming back. I hope so. If this is true, I will be back some June 24th.

When this river died, my brother and I began to explore new regions and my interest turned to salmon and steelhead. I became more focused on the coast where I now live and the fish that follow its rivers. As I learned about the state of salmon in California and other parts of the Pacific Coast, I became alarmed—perhaps a better word is obsessed—with trying to understand the complexities of the problem and the potential solutions.

This book is a celebration of salmon, but it is imbued with a warning that this great resource is imperiled and must be protected and nourished. The wild fish spawn in wild places. To reach these wild places, the fish must be able to travel freely up the streams and arrive where they can safely mate—and where their offspring can survive to repeat the cycle. When the wild fish are safe, the beautiful places they go to will also be safe. I want my child and her children to have such places in their future.

The Way Home

I HAVE ONLY TO CLOSE MY EYES and concentrate and I can see them coming home. The first time I tried to fish for salmon in a stream was twenty years ago on the Sacramento River in Northern California. A friend and I drove three hours from the San Francisco Bay Area to a dirt road that led to a rough parking place carved out of the thick streamside brush. We joined the dozen or so fishermen lining the bank and began to cast our heavy metal lures far out into the brown, roiling stream, a hundred feet wide where we stood. When I felt my lure bounce on the bottom, I rapidly reeled it in, as much hoping to snag a fish as to entice one to strike, though I didn't catch one that day.

I remember the first fish I saw jump out of the water. It seemed to explode from the surface, its red sides shimmering as it tried to swim in the air. Then it crashed back into the stream, an underwater treasure exposed momentarily to the light. I was startled and astonished. I imagined great numbers of salmon moving upstream, sometimes impatiently bumping into one another, a quick dash over a competitor sending a fish into the air. The water was thick with fish. They were most dramatic at sunset, when their silver bodies seemed to burst into the red evening glow.

Years later I am fishing for trout on the Itchen near Westminster Abbey in England. From where I am standing, the trees behind me have been carefully groomed so that I can backcast without getting hung up and send my little nymph into the water that flows through a patch of heavy grass in front of me. Real nymphs are washed off this grass to the brown trout waiting below. I have no strikes for my many casts. My mind starts to wander when suddenly a huge Atlantic salmon jumps out of the water right in front of me. My heart stops. I have no pretensions of catching it. Such a beast would break my line like an elephant snapping a twig. I am thrilled that one of these great, beautiful fish, and maybe more, still find these waters desirable and are still free. I run up the stream to find my guide, Jack, a kind old man with gentle eyes. I am a little kid now, so excited.

"Jack," I say, "you should have seen what I saw. A big salmon jumped right out of the pool just below the cut-off."

His face lights up with joy and he says with disappointment, "Damn, I wish I'd seen that fish."

The jumping fish mixed with the late light create a mystical feeling. I am in my underwear — I fell in the river and have forgotten to bring a change of clothes — on a cold night near Trondheim, Norway. But I am very content for the moment to sit in front of the fire drying out, watching the river and sipping whiskey with my friend Nils. It is now 11:30 p.m. and an enchanting calm has enveloped the river and its citizens. Other fishermen have made fires on the riverbank. The smoke rises straight up in the calm, still evening light.

In front of us in the quiet stretch of river that flows by the shack, a very large salmon breaks the water. Nils jumps up and casts a large silver lure across the river at him. A man dressed in overalls walks down from the other side. He has also spotted the giant salmon. His spoon splashes in the river. Nils says that this big salmon will keep other salmon from coming here, will chase them off. The salmon is red and ferocious with sharp teeth and a hooked jaw. He is a horny salmon, waiting for his women, and does not take the spoons.

The soft northern light seems to have entered the trees. It emanates from the stream. Each ripple catches this light and breaks it into colors that melt together to form new colors and shapes. The river dissolves into patches of light. The salmon become the light. They bring it up the river. They shine when they jump from the river into the dim glow. The boundaries are soft; trees join the water, the ripples touch the trees. The only crisp light is from the fires of the other fishermen. Our late-night campfires connect us river dwellers; we are surrounded by darkness, joined by these points of fire into a constellation. The great old salmon breaks once more from the ever-changing surface of the river, a flash of red-gold and puddles of silver. The sound of his splash is intense. Sounds are magnified,

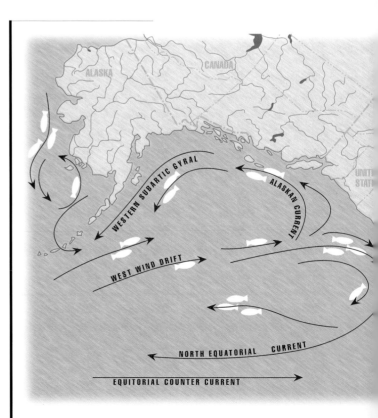

distinct; we can hear the twigs snapping from under the boots of the fishermen two hundred feet away as though they were at our own fire. Nils—is humming a song. "It is not just the fishes," he sings.

The experience is even better when the great fish is attached to the end of your fly line. I go up to Lake Creek in the Alaska Mountain Range to fly-fish for salmon. My guide puts me in the middle of the stream on a sandbar, facing a bank where the stream curves away from me along the other side to form a deep hole. Chinook salmon, some of them thirty pounds or more, swim along the bottom of this hole. I am thirty feet from the bank. I can easily cast my chartreuse fly far enough upstream so that it will have time to sink down deep to meet the fish. On the third cast, my line stops, the tip of the pole jerks toward the water and a fish begins to pull my line downstream with ease. A hundred feet below me, the fish comes right out of the water, as a rainbow trout might, but this is a three-foot fish. He just keeps going downstream and I know that it is foolish to try to stop him. He jumps again, now two hundred feet away. And then he jumps a third time—to freedom. I scream with joy and triumph. I have hooked one of these great fish. In the unlikely event that I had brought him in, I would have let him go anyway. I am glad he can continue his voyage with little strength lost. There will be many more like him coming up this stream. Throughout the summer and fall all the great salmon species will return.

Who among us has not marveled at the migration of salmon and wondered how they find their way home? These great fish, born in tiny streams throughout the Northwest, Northern California, Alaska, British Columbia and even Idaho, may travel thousands of miles from the place of their birth. For a year or more, depending on the species, they live in the ocean, furiously feeding on the rich abundance of the sea. Their flesh is shrimp pink. Some have become giants—over a hundred pounds. Then, mysteriously, they are called homeward.

How do they know how to get home from way out there in the deep sea where no scent of the parent stream can be detected? For many years it was assumed that salmon simply followed the major sea currents, which eventually brought them back to their natal stream.

There is more to the story, however. Unless there were more homeward bias in their movement than could simply be explained by the drift, salmon would have trouble covering the eighteen hundred-mile distance between their deep sea forages and their home stream in time to assemble for the upward migration. Even a little homeward bias would help them reach the parental streams at the appointed time. Evidence suggests that they learned the way home on their outward trip. Atlantic salmon released at sea who had not traveled down their natal streams returned to the nearest stream, not the one of their origin. The salmon must be attuned to the world in ways we can only imagine. Are they guided by the sun? Do they feel the magnetic fields of the earth? Do they follow the slope of the ocean floor or the line where waters of different salinity meet?

The major circulation of the surface waters in the North Pacific are also known ocean routes for several salmon species. Salmon entering the deep ocean from the Canadian coast or the Northwest United States might follow the Alaska current into the Western Subartic Gyral, eventually returning to the West Wind Drift, which would bring them close to home.

"I *wonder what keeps them going. They will die rather than give up. …They will jump and jump and jump until they perish of exhaustion or surmount whatever obstacles keep them from their upward journey.*"

R. Valentine Atkinson

However they manage to arrive at the mother stream, they all do so at about the same time and place each season. Their upward migration is regular and precise. Pictures of salmon painted on the walls of caves in Spain suggest that at least one early culture constructed its calendar year around the return of the salmon. Salmon fishermen book their favorite lodges at the same time each season, knowing that the run is likely to occur on that date.

We know something about how salmon find their way home once they are reasonably close to their parent stream. In the 1950s biologist Arthur Hasler proved that they could smell their way home. Hasler was influenced by the great German Nobel Laureate Karl von Frisch who opened his eyes to the importance of odors in animal behavior. Von Frisch had discovered that the skin of a minnow contains a chemical substance that causes other members of its school to disperse and hide. The biological advantage of this chemical is obvious: if a minnow is wounded by a predator and releases the substance, the other minnows will flee. Hasler's idea that fish can smell their native stream came to him when he was walking in the mountains of Utah. He wrote:

> We had driven …to my parental home in Provo, Utah. …As I hiked along a mountain trail in the Wasatch Range of the Rocky Mountains where I grew up, my reflections about the migratory behavior of salmon were soon interrupted by wonderful scents that I had not smelled since I was a boy. Climbing up toward the Alpine zone on the eastern slope of Mt. Timpanogos, I had approached a waterfall which was completely obstructed from view by a cliff; yet, when a cool breeze bearing the fragrance of mosses and columbine swept around the rocky abutment, the details of this waterfall and its setting on the face of the mountain suddenly leapt into my mind's eye. In fact, so impressive was this odor that it evoked a flood of memories of boyhood chums and deeds long since vanished from conscious memory.

Hasler decided that each stream contains a particular bouquet of fragrances to which salmon become imprinted before emigrating to the ocean. When it is time to return to the natal stream to spawn, they use these unique fragrances to get back home.

Salmon behavior cannot be explained entirely by their ability to home in on familiar scents. For instance, shortly after juveniles were introduced into a stream previously barren of salmon, adult salmon began returning to that stream. This suggests that adult salmon may smell their species and be drawn toward the smell.

As soon as the male salmon leaves the sea, he begins a formidable transformation: his lower jaw begins to enlarge and hook and oversized teeth appear. In some species his back transforms into a huge hump and he turns bright red. Sexual maturity is almost immediately followed by death, but the urge to mate stays with these males to the end. Males with frayed fins, skin torn from their flesh, mottled with fungus infections and sometimes even blind continue to exhibit courting behavior.

I wonder what keeps them going. They will die rather than give up. When dams are installed in rivers previously open to the fish, they will bash their heads senselessly against the concrete until they die. I marvel at the strength of their drive. They will jump and jump and jump until they perish of exhaustion or surmount whatever obstacles keep them from their upward journey. My drives are pitiful in comparison. The Romans, watching the fish jump in the tides of the reefs off the Atlantic coast, named them *salar* after their word for leapers. The great leapers. They are intoxicated by something in the final days of their life.

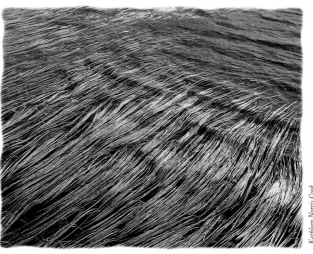

Kathleen Norris Cook

Each stream contains a particular bouquet of fragrances to which salmon become imprinted before emigrating to the ocean. They subsequently use the bouquet as a cue for identifying their natal tributary when they return from the sea. However, the draw of natal scents is not the only reason for the salmon's return. Shortly after juveniles were introduced into a stream previously barren of salmon, adult salmon were observed swimming up that stream, suggesting that the adults sensed their species and were drawn toward the smell.

R. Valentine Atkinson

Tom Mangelsen

The spawning of the salmon is an irresistible drama. On a Sunday afternoon nearly a hundred thousand people line the banks of the Issaquah Creek near Seattle to watch the fish spawn. Which female will gain the nesting site relished by others? Which suitor will triumph for the right to mate with a ripe female? Seldom are birth and death so connected. They watch fish die, their battered bodies floating downstream to dissolve into the water and create nutrients for the yet unborn. They watch the triumphant arrival of the ones who have finally made it home.

Tom & Pat Leeson

Salmon evolved to fit in with their natural surroundings — heavily forested river banks overhung with branches and lined with tangles of roots and fallen trees. The green and black coloration of young salmon blends in with this vegetation, which keeps the water cool, protects the salmon from predators and insures the growth of aquatic nutrients. Today silt and sediment from deforested slopes and logging roads fill the streams and sap the young salmon's strength. Those who manage to survive are smaller and sicker than those in untouched streams. The sediment abrades their gills and impairs their respiration. If salmon are to survive, we must preserve their natural environment.

Nancy Simmerman

R. Valentine Atkinson

Salmon swimming in the sea look very much alike, but once they come upstream they undergo a physical transformation unique to each species. The pinks develop a grotesque hump, the kings become bright red, the chum or dog salmon develop red and brown splotches. Their jaws enlarge and hook and oversized teeth appear. Only steelhead retain their silver, classic beauty since they will return to the sea after spawning.

There is a salmon hatchery located just below the Comanche Reservoir Dam about 100 miles east of San Francisco on the Mokelumne River. I went there one drizzly, cold day just before Christmas to watch the salmon spawning. Most of the salmon swim up into the hatchery, but a few spawn in the waters right below it. This stretch of shallow water flowing over a gravel bottom is like any other place where the salmon once spawned. The human visitors who come to watch the salmon in the stream are appreciatively quiet. I watch a big female king salmon, only a few feet in front of me out in the shallow stream, dig a deep pit in the gravel. The fish are very vulnerable during spawning time. Bears, eagles, otters, mink, wolves and humans can feed on them at will. I could easily scoop her out. The race to spawn must be efficient.

Swimming with her side flat to the bottom, the female or "hen" brushes away the gravel with strokes from her broad tail. Once finished, she deposits her eggs. The male salmon hovering nearby fertilizes them with a cloud of milt, and the hen covers them with gravel. The male deserts his mate as soon as he has finished fertilizing the eggs, but the female remains to defend her nest. The fertilized eggs are offered some protection by the gravel, but they are also fragile. If the gravel becomes covered with silt or is disturbed in any other way, if the water becomes too warm or the oxygen too thin, the eggs will die. Hence, the danger from logging and other destructive forces that damage the delicate ecosystem of the spawning habitat.

As I watch the female prepare her nest, I see a few small rainbow trout darting back and forth below her, waiting to gobble up her eggs. Carcasses of dead fish float down the deeper sections of the stream, others become caught between rocks or lie on the shore. A raven plucks out the eyes of one dead fish, and a crayfish scurries off with a piece of flesh. A group of buzzards assembled in the tall cottonwoods on the side of the stream wait their turn at the dinner table. As the light fades to pale yellow on the horizon, the buzzards seem even bigger and more alarming. Night falls, but the splashing of the mating fish continues with undiminished vigor. I walk off wishing that more of my eight million fellow citizens in the Sacramento and San Francisco Bay Areas could see this.

The eggs will hatch in a couple of months. The hatchlings will remain buried for three to four months in the gravel which protects them from predators. Finally, they will emerge as little fish several inches long called parr or fry. The fry are programmed to stay in protected areas and are disguised by their dark green color and distinct black vertical bars that blend in with streambank vegetation and the river bottom. They gobble plankton and aquatic insects that drift downstream in the current. Unfortunately, the odds are against these little fish. They are eaten by bigger fish, particularly the trout and squawfish in these waters, and by weasels, otters, birds and any other creatures that capture them.

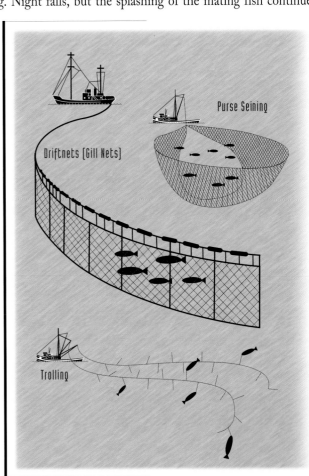

Purse Seining

Driftnets [Gill Nets]

Trolling

Imagine the difference between an ancient river surrounded by thick forest and a modern one whose banks are stripped of trees. In the ancient forest the fry were protected by overhanging branches and bushes, tangles of roots and fallen trees. There were deep holes where they could hide. Without this cover they are exposed to predators and, of course, heat.

Today silt and sediment from deforested slopes and logging roads fill the streams and sap the tiny salmon's strength. The fish who manage to survive are smaller and sicker than those in untouched forests. The sediment abrades their gills and impairs their respiration. To the extent that it clouds the water, it may even impair their ability to find food. Unfortunately, deforested streams are slow to recover. Even twenty years later the sediment level in such streams can be four times higher than before logging.

Within several months the small salmon of most species undergo a metamorphosis into smolts, the name for the seagoing stage of their development, and begin to move downstream. The dark marks disappear from their sides and the fish turn silver, a color that protects them in the ocean. They cease being territorial and form schools numbering in the thousands and embark en masse on the seaward journey.

The imprinting to a stream during the smolt stage can occur rapidly. Smolts released in a stream for only a few days will still return to it. This imprinting makes it possible to introduce salmon to streams they are not native to but, because of the environmental fine tuning of each group of salmon, their genetic makeup may not be optimal to survive in the new location.

How do the smolts move to the sea? In part the smolts are simply washed downstream. As the smolt develops, its swim bladder enlarges, increasing the fish's buoyancy and susceptibility to current. Smolts do not swim as well as fry in the current. They lose their sensitivity to low light, a result of the change in the composition of cells in the retina. This change may limit their ability to see the river bottom or orient themselves at night, again making them more sensitive to the current.

Drift nets and gill nets can nearly wipe out a salmon run, effectively snaring thousands of fish at a time. Dolphins and other marine animals also get caught in the mesh of the drift nets and drown. Purse seining is more selective, since the fish are encircled by the net rather than hooked by the gills. Though trolling is the most inefficient method of commercial fishing, the use of barbless hooks enables the release of unwanted fish with little harm to the animal.

In spite of these influences, the smolts also seem to know where they are going. For instance, the downstream migration of sockeye salmon through an intricate lake system follows a well-oriented, direct route.

The fish move downstream faster and more directly than the current can account for. A combination of passive drift and direct migration seems to be the most likely explanation for the seaward migration of the salmon.

Smolts evolved to move seaward through the rivers. Now, with many of their natal streams dammed, the fish must pass through long, slow backwaters where they become disoriented and vulnerable to freshwater predators such as squawfish.

When they arrive at the sea, they face even more dangers, some ancient and some modern. Sometimes nature brings an unexpected threat. In the early nineteen-nineties *El Niño*, a warm ocean current, shifted water through the Strait of Juan de Fuca up around Vancouver Island and along the coast of British Columbia. The warm water brought with it schools of rapacious mackerel. These fish fed freely on the young salmon who, because they begin their ocean life near the shore, are accustomed to few predators in the tidal zone. Sometimes the dangers are man-made, like the *Exxon Valdez* oil spill in Alaska that sent 250 thousand barrels of crude oil into the fertile waters of Prince William Sound, threatening 100 million juvenile salmon.

Until recently, the few adult salmon who survive these many threats lived in relative safety far out in the cold, dark northern Pacific Ocean. Then came the drift net fishermen. Drift nets consist of a series of plastic monofilament squares woven into 150-foot segments called tans. The tops of the tans are suspended from floats and their bottoms are weighted with lead. They are strung together in a straight line miles long.

Drift net fishermen let their nets out at night. This enables them to take advantage of the upward movement of the fish as they follow the animal plankton that rises after dark to feed on the plant plankton that lives near the water surface. The Asian drift net fishermen may let out thirty-five to fifty miles of nets. In the morning they slowly haul them in using huge winches. Enough nylon net is deployed each day by Japan, Korea and Taiwan to more than circle the earth.

The purpose of this drift net fishing is to catch squid. Prohibited animals, such as salmon and dolphins, are supposed to be released; yet nearly any animal that runs into the net will get caught, and most will die before they are hauled in. Although the squid boats are not allowed to fish in much of the salmon's sea territory, the salmon aren't aware of these artificial boundaries. They simply move around following the bait and are not likely to know that once they cross over a certain latitude and longitude, they may be caught. Evidence suggests that up to 250 thousand steelhead are being "stolen" each year by the drift net operations—about twenty percent of the entire West Coast steelhead fish population.

Thousands of tons of North American salmon of all species are being harvested by squid fleets working in the Bering Sea, and it is unlikely that we can ever stop the drift net operations from doing so. The only answer is to outlaw them! I have included an appendix in the back of the book that lists organizations involved with salmon conservation and preservation.

As they reach the mouths of rivers and their home streams, the next obstacle the adult salmon must survive is the commercial salmon fishermen. Most salmon are caught for commercial rather than recreational reasons, and these salmon feed millions of people. In Bristol Bay alone in one exceptionally good year, over forty million fish were caught.

There are three basic methods of commercial salmon fishing: gillnetting, purse seining and trolling. Commercial fishermen use gill nets about a quarter mile long and twenty to twenty-six feet deep that are released from a power drum at the stern of the boat. The mesh in these twine nets is about five inches square. Every one to three hours the net is reeled in and the fish—sometimes a hundred per set—are harvested.

Gillnetting in waters filled with fish about to enter a major river can decimate a run. During the peak migrations of sockeye in July, and pinks in August, the six hundred to seven hundred gill-netters working the Skeena Estuary in British Columbia can capture more than three-quarters of the salmon who originated in rivers draining into the estuary. Pictures of dead birds and seals wrapped in gill nets have made the Fishermen justifiably unpopular with the public. In 1992 the California voters passed Proposition 132, which essentially banned these nets from the California coast.

Purse seines are nets about twelve hundred to fourteen hundred feet long and are run by large vessels (forty-five to ninety feet). The tops of these nets are suspended from cork floats and the bottoms are pulled down by lead weights. The boat pulls

Nancy Simmerman

Sea lions and seals love salmon and steelhead and eat them with abandon, particularly when the spawners have assembled to swim up their natal streams. Eighty percent of wild spawners have seal or sea lion bites, and for every fish that escapes, many more are eaten. Commercial trollers bring up their salmon catches in a hurry before the seals can steal them. In some places there are so few fish left that the seals seem to be starving. Unless we can somehow slow the growth of the non-threatened seal and sea lion populations, we may lose them soon after the fish are gone to a painful death of slow starvation and disease.

the net into a circle and closes the bottom, much like pulling the drawstrings of a bag of marbles. Any fish encircled by the purse seines are caught. Where salmon are concentrated in schools or at the mouths of rivers, the purse seiners haul in a thousand or more salmon at a time. This fishing method is completely selective since all fish come on board alive, permitting the release of protected or endangered species.

Trolling is the least efficient type of commercial salmon fishing but maybe the most romantic. The troll boats use two long poles that are lowered away from the boat at about a forty-five-degree angle. Several fishing lines set at different depths come off each of the poles. Lures are then tied at various intervals along the line. Bells on the poles tingle when a fish is on and the fishermen then reel up the line using motor-driven winches. The leader with the fish on it is then pulled in by hand until the fish can be gaffed and brought aboard. Since barbless hooks are used, selected fish can be released with the majority surviving.

The commercial salmon fishermen, particularly those owning their boats and running a small crew, see themselves as rugged individualists protecting a lifestyle as endangered as the fish they pursue. They like scraping out a living on the ocean following the fish, masters of their day.

The number of fish the commercial fishermen are allowed to catch each year is set in the spring by various federal and state agencies. These catch limits are based on projected salmon returns to the rivers. When the projected returns are too optimistic and the commercial limits are set too high the results can be devastating as they were one year when regulators allowed too many fish to be caught off the California and Oregon coasts. The estimated coho population dropped from 1.2 million in 1991 to less than half a million a few years later.

The catch limits, reflected by how long the season will be open, are hotly debated at meetings where public input is sought. The lives of the fish and the livelihood of the fishermen are at stake. Unfortunately, in recent years there have been too many commercial fishermen vying for far too few fish.

The great journey of the salmon involves vulnerability from beginning to end. Mindlessly, the fish cross counties, states and nations. They are desired by commercial fishermen, sports fishermen and a host of wild creatures. Since they wander from mountains to oceans, the condition of their environment reflects our care of the world. Their future is only as safe as we make it.

In places where the runs have dwindled, much finger pointing goes on: the commercial fishermen blame the loggers and farmers; the recreational fishermen blame the commercial fishermen; everyone blames the dams, the seals and the Japanese. Protection of wild steelhead and salmon will require sacrifices from all the interests that compete over water, energy and forests; and from all of us who fish, be we individuals or commercial operations. If the salmon are to survive, loggers will have to take fewer logs, more water will have to flow naturally to the sea and hydroelectric dams will have to generate less energy. Commercial and recreational fishermen will have to take smaller catches, and the recreational fishermen will have to pay more money for the privilege of fishing.

Tom & Pat Leeson

Fishermen can bring in a huge catch using purse seines. These long nets
are weighted down with lead and suspended from cork floats. Schooling
fish swim into the enclosure and are captured when the net is pulled into a
circle and closed around them. Then the catch is hauled up into the boat
using winches.

Given the nature and the importance of the problem, some environmental groups have recommended an idea that I find very appealing. They have suggested that the President appoint a Salmon-Keeper, a person with the authority to develop a comprehensive plan to protect and restore the wild salmon and steelhead. This plan would need to be international and deal with such touchy issues as drift nets, catch limits and inspections of boats fishing in waters outside the United States. Perhaps the Salmon-Keeper could also appoint River-Keepers, at least one for each of the major rivers. The River-Keepers could monitor the life and ecology of their assigned waterway and also have the power and resources to protect and restore them.

Local efforts can also make a big difference. San Francisquito Creek is a little stream that originates somewhere in the Santa Cruz Mountains above the Stanford University campus. It runs down past the Stanford Linear Accelerator, the Stanford golf course and downtown Palo Alto to the Bay. Although this stream is only a mile from where I sit writing this, I had no idea that steelhead ran so close to home until I learned of the following. A few years ago Jim Johnson, a local conservationist and member of the Friends of San Francisquito Creek, noticed that El Palo Alto, a giant redwood tree and the namesake of the town, had increased its tilt. While monitoring the tree, he noticed two large steelheads lying dead below a concrete stream stabilization dam built to protect a railroad track. One of the fish was bloodied from its upward struggles, and the other, a female, had died from some other cause. The sight of the fish inspired him with the idea that others might have made it upstream. Was it possible that native fish still existed in San Francisquito and its tributaries? This seemed unlikely since the creek dried up in the summer; but its tributaries, fed by springs, ran year round before disappearing into gravel at lower elevations. Believing that steelhead might be able to survive in such streams, he found what might be three varieties of steelhead smolts. These steelhead spent their three freshwater years in the foothills and were released to the ocean by the winter rains. Their ancestors had returned in these same high winter waters, spawned and dashed back to sea.

The discovery of these smolts inspired a number of people to try to open San Francisquito Creek and its tributaries to the returning fish. They found the possibility of restoring the fish runs so exciting that they were willing to make costly concessions about when and how they would use water from the little stream. Obstructions blocking the fish were removed or circumvented.

The Coyote Creek Riparian Station and Community Creek Watch, along with Johnson, who has since become San Francisquito's Stream-Keeper, have begun a habitat monitoring project on the stream. Volunteers measure a number of aspects of its ecology. Hundreds of people touch and are touched by the soul of this creek.

Curious, I walk over to El Palo Alto. There I find a plaque recognizing that this tree "lived here at the time of the signing of our Constitution." In fact, this tree lived here at the time of the signing of the Magna Carta. Someday it may be possible to sit next to this tree and watch steelhead come up the fish ladder and disappear toward the foothills. If we help them, the fish will come home.

Damming the Wild Streams

THE RUGGED BEAUTY OF THE CALIFORNIA coastline north of Long Beach is created by coastal mountains that drop abruptly into the deep, blue ocean. This confrontation of land and sea has created a vast, ever-changing vista of coves, beaches and rocks sculpted by the tides. The land has been further shaped by the huge seasonal rainfalls in these mountains. These rains have created great rivers that, over the centuries, produced canyons and estuaries and myriad zones for the diversification of life forms that further altered the environment. A hundred years ago salmon may have entered most of these streams as far south as Long Beach. Silver salmon and steelhead still enter the streams along the Santa Lucia Range on the Big Sur Coast.

I drive down to the Big Sur River from Palo Alto to see if any steelhead have come into the stream this year, though four years of drought have dried up most of the smaller streams along the coastal ranges and a fish run is unlikely in any of them. Still, any excuse to take this beautiful drive.

I know I have arrived at Andrew Molera State Park where the Big Sur River enters the ocean when I see the Point Sur Lighthouse a few miles to the north. I follow the trail down to the beach. I can tell by the size of the delta at the state park that the stream must have often overflowed its boundaries and changed course many times, moving from one side of the valley to the other after a huge runoff. In this dramatic spot the Santa Lucia Mountains rise up 4,724 feet to the Venta Cone only a few miles inland from the sea. For most of the year, these are dry mountains clothed in desert plants, the river dropping precipitously from them to the ocean.

The Big Sur River originates twenty miles or so up into these mountains. Just before it enters the ocean it runs along sharp black rocks until, only a few inches deep, it joins the sea. To its left a smooth, sandy beach stretches in a slow curve to Cooper Point three miles away.

The river is too shallow for the salmon and steelhead to enter it this year. I imagine that they are waiting in the deep water offshore, swimming expectantly back and forth like dogs just before the hunt. If the river never rises, and the steelhead survive the ever-more-frequent assault from seals, they will reabsorb their eggs or milt and swim off to return another year. These steelhead are exceptionally hardy. They evolved under conditions of low river flow, can withstand water temperatures of up to eighty degrees, and are quicker to dash up rivers from the ocean than more northern California steelhead. In spite of their genetic vigor, the fish native to this river are in a precarious situation. If a drought lasts four or five years, longer than the fish's life span, the native population will never be able to spawn and will become extinct. If that should happen, in a very wet year some befuddled salmon or steelhead born in another stream might happen to wander up the Big Sur and start a new population.

I decide to walk up along the riverbank to see if some determined steelhead might have already entered the river. I take a step off the sandy beach, past the blue grass and the beach grass and the dark crimson flowers of the sand verbena, and I am enclosed by brush. These riparian forests, which once covered large sections of central California, are now only found in state parks and a few other unmolested miles of riverbank. At one time all the major California rivers carried huge amounts of silt down from the mountains. This silt and sediment formed levees that on the larger rivers often rose up ten to thirty feet above the normal water level and extended back several miles from the river's edge.

Because of the rich soil nutrients and available water, these levees were once rampant with growth. They often became junglelike, particularly in summer. The forest I am walking through now is reminiscent of those times. Trees from the surrounding hills drop seeds into the water, which find fertile ground in the levee and soon produce cottonwoods, box elders, Oregon Ash, various types of willows, live oaks, sycamores, bay trees, alders, dogwood and firs. Shrubs like buttonbush, honeysuckle, wild rose, coffeeberry and elderberry grow in abundance.

The foliage of the trees and shrubs around me merges together into an almost impenetrable mass. The ground is covered by fallen limbs and other debris, berry and rose vines, poison oak and poison ivy, saplings, and flowers. I am alone except for the many birds playing in the trees and the monarch butterflies that flutter through the brush like bright flying spots of orange. Little offshoots from the main trail go to the river's edge. Why, I wonder? These are people-made trails. What were the people looking for? Trying to get closer to the river, I follow each trail but my progress is surprisingly difficult. The foliage overgrows the river's edge, making it nearly inaccessible. A hawk flying above me might see that I am only a stone's throw from the beach and the stream, yet I feel as if I am in a jungle. In Alaska I had the same somewhat suffocating feeling. A sense of danger nags at my consciousness, but what is the danger here? There are deer ticks infested with Lyme disease hanging on this brush waiting for a passing mammal. The water is undoubtedly filled with giardia, the omnipresent protozoa that cause intestinal distress for those unlucky enough to imbibe them. I hope some rattlesnakes and a few scorpions still survive to add a taint of dangerous thrill.

I follow each subtrail to the river's edge. One leads to a stretch of water deep enough to hold a fish. To see the river bottom, I must climb out on the white trunk of an ash tree that grows out over the river. Suddenly, the water moves, its surface rippling in the characteristic manner of a large fish fleeing upstream. I see only waves as the reflection of the trees and sky break into pieces of silver and blue on the surface of the water—gentle undulations. I freeze. What a great pleasure it is to sneak toward an unknown water and look for fish! What joy to peek through the brush and see the dark form of a great salmon waiting at the bottom—even better when you have a chance to catch it. What a challenge to consider how to approach this great fish, how to cast and what fly to use. From where I am now, however, I am highly visible to the fish, who would perceive me as an awkward, stumbling mass creeping out on a thin branch above him. The water is calm again, but when I move along the branch, the surface of the water ripples once more. This movement seems different from the undulations I saw moments before. Have my expectations altered my vision and created the fish I wanted to see? There is only one way to find out—to go upstream and peer into each section of the river. My stealth turns frantic as I rush along the main trail, taking each little offshoot, trying to cover as much of the river's edge as possible in the hope of glimpsing a fish. I see no fish but, regaining my composure and walking more leisurely, I see California poppies, sea figs with pink flowers, ox-eye daisies, cat's ear, bees, jumping spiders, a red-tailed hawk, berries, coots, and the mountains rising up into the blue, blue sky.

Though I spot no migrating salmon or steelhead, I am not disappointed. This little venture was partly an excuse to drive down to Big Sur. I walk back to the beach, lie next to the river, listen for fish and read *Hieronymous Bosch and the Oranges of Big Sur.*

A week after my Big Sur trip it started to rain and just kept on raining. The rain came in great gushes straight off the Pacific and poured down in the thirsty Santa Lucia Mountains. On the day it stopped, I decided to go back to Andrew Molera State Park to see if I could spot a few steelhead or salmon moving upstream. I also took along my fly rod and reel, just in case. When I arrive, the ranger, a modern, public relations-minded type, is being interviewed by a reporter carrying a portable tape recorder. I ask the ranger if I can fish here.

"Nope," he says, "at least not until the general trout season opens."

"Have the steelhead come in?" I ask.

"I am sure they have. When the water clears on Saturday, you'll be able to see them in the deep holes of the park up there." He gestures toward Pfeiffer Park.

I walk down the trail again beside the now-roiling, muddy river. The world has changed. The brown hills have turned bright green. Even the desert scrub on the mountains is green, with spots of blue lupine peeking out. It's as if all this color was waiting just beneath the surface for a chance to explode.

I am almost overcome by butterflies. Walking toward the river, engrossed in salmon thoughts, I enter a grove of huge eucalyptus trees. The trees grow in a broad arc and their trunks are black from a fire that spared their upper boughs. The butterflies are like little patches of bright orange playing in the sunlit shafts penetrating through the trees. Monarchs migrate down the Pacific Coast, often resting in great masses in such eucalyptus groves, out of harm's way. In the Monarch Grove in Santa Cruz, they hang in great bunches like branches of dead leaves.

Tom Montgomery

Big Sur, the meeting place of mountains and sea, boasts some of the world's most beautiful coves, beaches and rugged rocks. The seasonal rains create great rivers that salmon enter to spawn and die. When young salmon hatch from the eggs in these mountain streambeds the cycle begins anew. Hidden within the eddies of shadowed waterways the young fry begin their journey to the ocean.

Kathleen Norris Cook

Kathleen Norris Cook

Just before I reach the river, I see the quick movements of tiny animals darting through a puddle in the path in front of me. I think they must be tadpoles, but when I get down on my hands and knees to examine the creatures, I see that they are little fish. On closer inspection they appear to be minnows. How did they get here? The river does not seem to have overflowed, nor the tide to have come up this high. Rained down from the sky—an unsolved mystery.

At the mouth of the river, now too deep to cross, two surfers are studying a tide chart. I study the water but see no salmon moving upstream. The salmon would have no trouble going up this river now, but to do so they would have to cross over a gravel bank, and for a moment their backs would stick out of the water. The surfers say they have not seen any fish. I walk back to the car.

I was not able to get back to the Big Sur River that weekend to see the spawning steelhead, but I had a good opportunity to go to the origins of another winter steelhead stream. My daughter Megan's friend had asked her dad to take her camping as part of her recent birthday celebration and had invited Megan and me along. I couldn't imagine my daughter or many other eleven-year-old girls in California wanting to go camping on their birthday—unless they could pitch a tent in the local mall—so I seized the opportunity, particularly because the girls wanted to go to Portola State Park, which sits on the origins of Pescadero Creek. The seaside entrance of this stream had been blocked by sand, but I knew that ten inches of rain had fallen recently in the Santa Cruz Mountains. If any fish were still around, they would be heading up the river for the spawning grounds. By the time of our weekend camping trip, the water would be clear.

Those wishing a private experience with nature in California need to choose the off-hours and seasons: early in the morning before the masses are on the roads, in the early spring when the world is wet and muddy, late in the fall when cold weather and the possibility of an early snow frightens the fainthearted, or in early March after ten inches of rain have fallen and more is on the way. When we arrive, we and half a dozen other dedicated campers have Portola State Park to ourselves. We camp on the side of Peters Creek in a grove of old-growth redwoods that rise hundreds of feet above us. The smoke from our fire curls slowly upward, weaving into the trees, mixing with the sunlight.

In the morning the girls want to hike to Tip-Toe Falls where they can run back and forth into the cave behind the falls, slide down the muddy trail and in other ways get wet and dirty. The trail we follow goes down to the main stream, now no more than twenty feet across and half a foot deep. Judging by debris on the bank, I can see that the river had been two feet higher a few days before. The rain has come and gone like water in a flushed toilet. The footbridge has been washed out, and we must cross by hopping from one stone to another. I see no fish in this little stream. On the opposite side the trail heads up the hillside, steep and dark beneath the tall trees. We walk for about a mile along the ridge above the stream, the thick foliage making it impossible for us to see very far. Suddenly, the trail opens up where a rock slide has knocked down the trees. I pause to look down at Pescadero Creek, now sixty feet below us. And there in the green, clear water two steelhead have joined for their spawning dance. I stand transfixed—too long, because the girls have run on ahead with the other dad. I am irresistibly drawn to these fish. I walk up the trail to where it drops down to the water. About a quarter of a mile down the stream, at the tail end of a deep pool, I can see ripples caused by stirring fish. A large dead redwood has fallen along the stream at the base of the pool, providing cover for my observations, and I peek over its edge. A big male—maybe twenty inches long—is making amorous advances to a smaller female—maybe eighteen inches. She is simply swimming leisurely in the water, not yet digging a spawning bed. The male continues to approach her, sometimes turning on his side and making rapid sideways pelvic thrusts as through he were releasing milt. Then an even bigger male enters the pool. The first male darts after the interloper. The two swirl furiously around the female, and the newcomer is chased off, only to reappear a minute later. The two dash in quick circles at the tail of the pool and once again the first male chases the intruder off. The female hardly leaves her spot.

On the third attempt to steal the female, the larger interloping male is driven to the very end of the pool where the water flows out over gravel rocks to the next water hole a hundred feet below. In escaping from the first male, the interloper actually swims downstream for a foot or two. He pauses to gain his strength, but he has gone too far. When he turns to reenter the slow waters of the riffle, his broad body, perpendicular to the current like a little dam, is swept even further downward into alarmingly shallow water. Suddenly, this great fish is stranded—half in and half out of the stream. He pauses, his mouth underwater, his gills working furiously as though to catch his breath. He tries again to go upstream. I see before me in miniature the ancient epic struggle of these fish as the steelhead tries to move upward in water too shallow to support him.

This struggle becomes very painful for me to watch. Perhaps he is too tired to go on. Perhaps the water level has dropped since he entered the main pool, so that now he flounders where shortly before there was safe water. When he starts to move again, he chooses the wrong side of the stream and is soon back in the shallow water. Trying to land in deeper water, he thrashes his body back and forth. A little pool a few inches deep next to a rock offers him temporary salvation. Here, sitting quietly, he looks almost like a rock himself. Then he tries again, but his attempt only sends him further downstream. As he thrashes to find a deeper flow, I actually see him bounce a few feet to where the creek divides into two branches, one small and one very small. Certainly the latter will be his death.

At this point I feel an uncontrollable urge to rescue the fish—to carry him back up to the deep, safe pool. He rests in the little pool, appearing very weak, but at least his head is pointed upstream. If this is nature's way, a seemingly big and fit fish will lose out to a smaller one. I wonder if maybe there would be an advantage for smaller fish during a cycle of severe drought where greater size might make returning to the natal stream through shallow water impossible. Then I think of those great lost steelhead contained in this fish's genes. I also just feel sorry for him. So I walk down to give him a lift. Perhaps the sight of this huge beast lumbering toward him, or a longer rest, gives him added strength. When he sees me, he swims forward with great speed and strength, part fish, part bird, almost jumping over the rocks, only half in the water, and is soon in the deeper, safer, but still shallow waters of the other creek branch. I give up on rescuing him and simply resume watching. It is not long before he has worked himself back to the shallow stream he just escaped from. I have had enough of interloping.

About this time I can see a new pod of steelhead making their way up the little creek to the original pool. There are half a dozen travelers, all of them at least two feet in length. The sight of them fills me with another nearly uncontrollable urge—the longing to become a lawbreaker. The fit comes upon me as I see the mating male I have been watching open his mouth to engulf a mayfly and hear the rear guard of spawners splashing upstream. I think, "Would a little tussle with a friendly fisherman casting

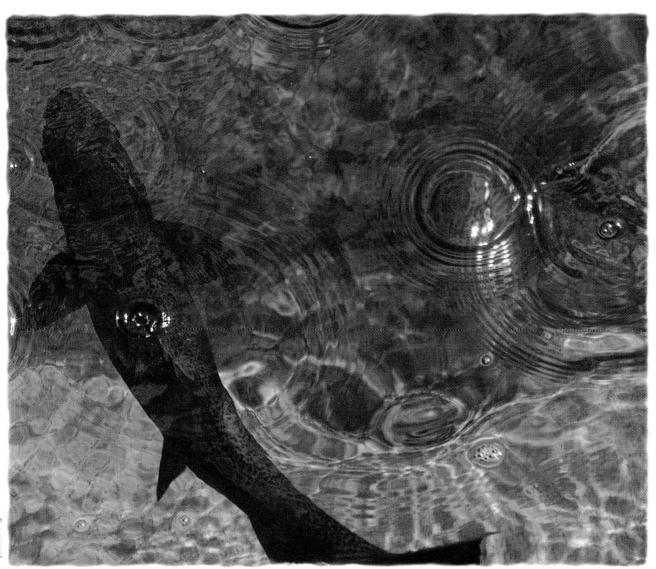

John Running

a fly in the scum flowing down the center of this pool make any difference to anyone?" I add up the cost of having my fly rod and gear confiscated and a hefty fine imposed—I am only a thousand feet from the ranger station plastered with "no fishing" signs—yet this would be about the same cost as a trip up to the Klamath River to catch fish no bigger than these. I feel a twitch in my left wrist, but I know I have interfered enough already. Maybe casting my rod wouldn't make a difference, maybe it would. This male has shown the strength—and courage—to make it up here first in line. He has chased off at least one bigger male and now has a somewhat interested female lined up for his progeny. Trying to get off my hook would only wear him out further. It would use up strength he might well need in contests with those big fish coming up the stream now. All things considered, I decide to let him be; but don't ask what I would have done if I'd had my rod and fishing were legal.

Central California is a flat, ancient sea bed, fifty miles across and four hundred miles long, framed by the Sierra Nevada Mountains to the east and the smaller Coastal Range to the west. Two major rivers, the Sacramento to the north and the San Joaquin to the south, flow through this valley, eventually joining together in the Sacramento Delta where the fresh water from the mountains mixes with the tidal ocean water. These two major rivers once provided millions of salmon access to thousands of miles of spawning grounds. After spending a few years in the ocean, the fish would pass by what is now the Golden Gate Bridge and swim north through San Francisco, San Pablo, and Suisun Bays until they eventually reached fresh water. By 1990 one species of these salmon—the winter-run salmon—had come perilously close to extinction, so close that it was declared an endangered species. The fate of this species seems to reflect the future of so many other salmon and steelhead runs that I decided to try to understand what had happened and what could be done about it.

Salmon return to spawn in all seasons. Most spawn in the fall of the year, but some return in the winter, a few in the spring, and some even in summer, although the latter two runs are probably extinct on the Sacramento River. A few kinds of salmon return after only one year in the sea, but most come back after two or three years—some big fish even after four or five years. In a dry year if the rains start in December or January, the winter-run fish may stand the best chance of finding water deep enough to sustain their eggs. These salmon have a unique spawning pattern. They enter the Sacramento River in the winter, and swim upstream 280 miles to the waters below Keswick Dam where they stay until they spawn in the fall. This diversity of behavior is part of the wonder of the salmon species and probably accounts for its survival in the face of such great efforts by humankind to block its return to the spawning grounds.

The winter-run salmon are only a tiny part of the whole Sacramento River salmon pool. In all, an estimated 120 to 180 thousand salmon enter the Sacramento River each year, although these numbers are still a tenth of what they were a hundred years ago.

The decline of the salmon runs began in the latter half of the nineteenth century when

Dams on the major salmon rivers of California have resulted in the decimation of salmon runs in that state, nearly wiping out some species. Though bypass devices such as fish ladders and traps have been constructed to help the salmon get beyond the dams, few of these have been successful. Fish hatcheries located near many dams capture spawning salmon and strip them of eggs and milt.

commercial fishing for salmon accelerated. Gill nets and seines were operating on the Sacramento and San Joaquin Rivers and in Suisun and San Pablo Bays. When the world's first salmon cannery was set up in Sacramento, the fish were soon stripped from the rivers. In 1882 twelve million pounds of salmon were caught, mostly from these two rivers, but only two million pounds were caught a decade later.

Unfortunately, even as the fishermen realized the dangers of overfishing the rivers, so much damage had been done to the habitat through hydraulic mining for gold that the numbers of salmon never fully recovered. In 1884 hydraulic mining in the California foothills was declared a public nuisance and banned. This technique used streams of high-pressure water to wash soil into sluices where the gold would settle in riffles allowing for easy separation from the gravel. It stripped away the surface vegetation making the land susceptible to erosion. Scars from hydraulic mining still blemish many rivers in the California foothills a hundred years after the mining was stopped, and they will still be here a hundred years from now.

Then came the dams. The dams were built to control the water in the Central Valley, creating an agricultural paradise out of semiarid desert. A seabed in ancient times, the Central Valley was gradually covered with sediment from the surrounding mountains. This sediment became fertile soil, but the soil was of little use to farmers without water. Rain falls in this area only between November and March. Then the valley turns hot and dry. Plants wilt and 100-degree days are common. The gold miners traveling to the California foothills passed a yellow grassland in the summertime and a vast marsh in the winter and spring. Millions of antelope, deer and a good number of bears and other creatures roamed these grasslands, and the marsh teemed with wildlife. Millions of ducks, geese and cranes spent the winter there. Beginning in the 1930s the rivers were dammed and an intricate maze of levees, weirs, canals and ditches was developed to divert water from California's

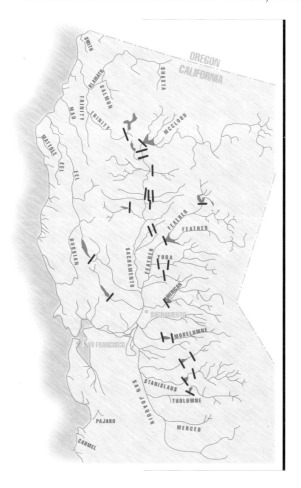

streams and distribute it over most of the Central Valley. This system controlled floods and irrigated hundreds of thousands of acres. The result was a farmer's paradise, producing enough food to feed one-quarter of America.

I have often driven up Route 99, the major Central Valley highway, past seemingly endless fields of almond, apricot and apple trees, all laid out in straight rows that converge in the distance. In the springtime these trees blossom into a vast layer of white and pink flowers that cover an equally intense layer of yellow clover blooming on the ground below. Grape vines, rice fields, tomatoes—vast patches of these and many other vegetables and grains and vines weave together into a great quilt covering much of the valley. This cornucopia looks a lot different from a fish's perspective. Where once there were over sixty-five hundred miles of streams available for spawning, now there are fewer than three hundred.

R. Valentine Atkinson

R. Valentine Atkinson

A joy of fishing is watching the surface of the water changed by the

fish. The effect of a jumping salmon or steelhead is breathtaking and dra-

matic but sometimes the effects are more subtle.

Rancho Llano Seco is one example of how generous, far-sighted people can both protect and restore wildlands and wildlife habitats. This eighteen hundred-acre refuge along the banks of the Sacramento River has remained intact since it was deeded as a Mexican land grant. The ranch had been privately owned and kept off-limits to all except the owners and employees. Most of the land has not been developed. As a result, the ranch remains a riparian forest and permanent marsh, with the river allowed to flood the land, a reflection of what the whole river plain was once like. The project is a joint venture with the U.S. Fish and Wildlife Service, the California Wildlife Conservation Board, the Nature Conservancy and a number of other agencies.

R. Valentine Atkinson

R. Valentine Atkinson

Then came the drought. By 1992 five years of drought in California made an emergency out of a crisis. Salmon died of hyperthermia in the low, hot waters of their native streams, and the winter-run chinook salmon came perilously close to extinction. Even when the drought ended in 1993, few winter-run chinook entered the Sacramento River. Their survival as a distinct population of salmon is uncertain.

Californians are so optimistic and have such short memories. When the rains come and the reservoirs fill up, talk of drought is replaced by complaints of too little sunshine. What people don't want to contemplate is that droughts will return, population will continue to increase, and water shortages will become more and more acute with time. John Steinbeck wrote in *East of Eden*:

> *There were dry years too and they put a terror in the valley. The water came in a thirty-year cycle. …And it never failed that during the dry years the people forgot about the rich years, and during the wet years they lost all memory of the dry years.*

Who owns the water and how it will be distributed is a great debate for the next century and it will determine the fate of the salmon and many other animal species in the Central Valley. There are three major constituencies competing for California's water—the cities, the farms and the environment. So far in this century, the agricultural industry has controlled most of the water. Even with California's vast population growth, eighty percent of the water is still used for agriculture. This eighteen billion-dollar industry is one of the largest and most important in the state.

The highly subsidized water in the northern part of the valley goes to nurture mainly four crops—rice, alfalfa, cotton and irrigated pasture land. The rice growers have drawn the most heat because their situation seems most ridiculous and unfair—growing a monsoon crop in a desert.

We have backed ourselves—our world, our fish and our wildlife—into some tough decisions. Are the pleasant green lawns in front of our houses less important than a stretch of forest in the mountains? When basic resources such as water are depleted, there are no simple solutions. Overpopulation is the greatest threat to the loss of our wild habitat. To meet the food needs of these vast populations, more and more agricultural production is needed, and the price in lost natural resources becomes steeper and steeper. Population control must be part of the solution.

Meanwhile, a few determined Sacramento winter salmon try to make their way up to the spawning grounds in the stretch of water between the town of Red Bluff and Shasta Dam fifty miles upstream. This massive dam, finished in 1945, wiped out half of their spawning grounds. There is no way for the salmon to get past this six hundred-foot-high concrete slab, but they could spawn in the waters below the dam, at least until 1964. Then another dam was built just below Red Bluff, forty miles south of Redding, to divert water from the Sacramento River into two canals that transport water for agriculture.

The Red Bluff Diversion Dam is a rather innocuous-looking structure, despite its having nearly wiped out a species. It is about twelve feet high, a few hundred feet long, and built in sections that can be raised to let the water flow downstream more freely. It has a fish ladder that has been hard for the fish to find and climb. The dam was built with two long, gravel-lined ditches that the fish were supposed to use instead of their natural spawning grounds. Unfortunately, the salmon didn't want to spawn

Unless California curbs its appetite for water, shifts water use or finds new supplies, shortages will be inevitable, and the salmon and the healthy environment they need for their survival will remain in danger. Wily politicians will revive old dreams to forever inscribe their names and their projects upon the face of mother earth. Many bold designs have been proposed. One of the projects planned would take water from the Trinity Mountain streams on the Northern California coast and divert it to the Central Valley, further endangering the salmon and steelhead runs in these rivers. A much bolder plan would bring water to California all the way from the Yukon and other Canadian rivers. These changes would wreak havoc on the environment, but another drought might quickly change priorities.

R. Valentine Atkinson

in such a treeless, soulless place. They instinctively seek places where irregular banks and heavy forest growth cool the water and provide escape from predators.

Efforts to save the winter salmon have focused on this structure, which kills the salmon coming and going. Because the fish were not able to get up the ladders to the fish trap where they could be caught and moved upstream or taken to the hatchery, the gates are now opened from December to April, allowing the fish to bypass the ladders and move directly upstream. An attempt was made to cut down on the squawfish living below the diversion dam. Young salmon tumbling out of the turbulent waters under the dam are easy prey for the squawfish, which gobble them up like corn strewn in a chicken coop.

Plans were made to release greater flows from Lake Shasta to lower the water temperature in the spawning grounds above Red Bluff. A more far-reaching plan is to lay a pipe deep along the bottom of Lake Shasta to bring the coldest water out to the fish.

Some of the adult salmon were captured in the ladders and transferred to the Coleman Hatchery where they could be reared more safely. This hatchery was built in 1942 to help reduce salmon loss from blocked habitat. It is hidden away in a little valley on the bank of Battle Creek, a tributary to the Sacramento. The valley is peaceful and unexploited, except for a few citizens practicing the American right to discard junked cars, refrigerators, tires, and tractor parts in their front yards.

The hatchery produces about 14 million chinook salmon and 1.5 million steelhead each year. The hatching process is quite simple, although it has evolved over years of experimentation. A little dam blocks Battle Creek at the entrance to the hatchery. The seven thousand or so fall chinook salmon and steelhead that return each year are forced to swim up a fish ladder into a holding pond. The fish are then crowded into elevator baskets that convey them to the spawning building. There they are killed, and the eggs of one female are stripped into a bucket and mixed with milt taken from two males. The eggs are then taken to the hatchery building—essentially a huge shed. One-half of the building is filled with rows of plastic trays, stacked one on top of the other in cabinets. Cold water flows over the trays, keeping the temperature ideal for the embryos and the fry. After several months the fry are transferred to long raceways where they are fed specially formulated fish food consisting of mostly fish meal (dust to dust) supplemented with vitamins and minerals. As the salmon grow, they are transferred to larger raceways. When they are about three and one-half inches long, they are released into Battle Creek where they make their long voyage to the sea. Maybe one in two thousand will return three or four years later.

Why do so few return? Many die en route to the ocean. Some get eaten by squawfish or bass, lost in a rice paddy, or succumb to the toxic affects of pollution. Many are taken by commercial fishermen, some by recreational fishermen, and many others are eaten by seals. In 1994 the projected salmon runs were so low that the California commercial fishing season was severely curtailed.

Restoring the streams the salmon travel to their spawning areas may be difficult but it is possible. It would make a big difference to the salmon if we could at least ensure adequate water flows in the rivers to support them at the various stages of their lives. The city folks, the farmers and the other water-users will need to pay more for their water. Commercial catches must be severely curtailed in the future. Those who fish for recreation should *release* the fish.

And maybe, if we are wise, generous and lucky, we can still save the Sacramento winter-run chinook. These fish symbolize a bigger issue: our callous disregard for natural things. This species, like its relatives, has swum up this river since the Ice Age. By protecting it we can give something to our descendants, not only the salmon but a world that retains its natural places.

THE RAIN COAST

ON NOVEMBER 7, 1804 WILLIAM CLARK, SENT by Thomas Jefferson with his partner, Meriwhether Lewis, to explore the Louisiana Purchase and Pacific Northwest, exclaimed as he finally arrived at the mouth of the Columbia River: "Ocean in View! O! The joy." I want to imagine what this moment was like for them. Unfortunately, on the day I have chosen for the drive, a typhoon is ramming the coast. Eighty-mile-an-hour winds are thrashing the huge spruce trees. The wipers are unable to clear the water from the windshield and the road is slick with debris. I worry that a large tree may be down ahead. I want to reach the ocean, but I decide it is better to stop at Naselle, about twelve miles from the coast. It rains all night—six inches worth—and the winds reach 100 miles an hour.

The storm dies down by morning. During the night the Naselle has overrun its banks—what I thought was a pond behind the motel is now a chocolate riverbank. Water and lights are out. We have been temporarily restored to more natural conditions, but the efficient road crews have already cleared trees from the highway, and it is easy passage to the Lewis and Clark campsite at the mouth of the Columbia. As I pass by the thick forests that cover the gentle mountains, I see entire sectors that have been clear-cut by loggers, leaving nothing but trunks and rubble. This is the basic geography and economy of this part of the world and one reason why so many of the salmon runs are in trouble. These clear-cut patches are ugly and ruin the pattern of the landscape, but, aesthetics aside, they also alter the ecology of streams. In *The Good Rain*, published in 1990, Timothy Egan writes about his visit to Deer Creek, a stream about sixty miles northeast of Seattle and a feeder to the Stillaguamish, one of the greatest steelhead streams in the world. He says:

> I've never seen anything like this—a cancerous canyon five hundred feet across, two thousand feet long and eight hundred feet deep. More than a million cubic yards of debris have slid into the river. Five years ago, this was a gentle forest slope. Then, the Georgia Pacific Timber Company clearcut most of the trees in the watershed. Now, the land will not hold water.

The rain that nurtures the fish also nurtures the trees. The Northwest coastline from the Gulf of Alaska well into California is steep and abrupt. The even temperatures and heavy rainfall are produced by the Japanese Current, which begins between Eastern Micronesia and the Philippines and flows in a northerly direction along the coast of Asia. The current is forced eastward by the Aleutian Mountain chain in Alaska and the shallows of the Bering Sea, then moves south along the North American shore. As it flows along the coast, the current releases warm vapor, which is blown shoreward. The warm air is forced upward against the coastal mountains until it drops as rain. Many coastal areas receive over 100 inches a year.

The Columbia River's mouth is so vast that it is hard to tell where it ends and the ocean begins. It drains over fifteen thousand miles of streams in an area the size of France. A quarter of a million cubic feet of water pass by this spot every second—enough water to give everyone on earth a glass of water every few minutes. It was not until May 1792 that the Europeans were able to enter the Columbia River, when Captain Gray took his ship, the *Columbia Redid,* past the great current at its mouth. Once into the river, he encountered the Chinook natives, who lived on a little peninsula that has since washed away. I stand close to this spot, looking seaward and envisioning how it must have seemed to the Chinooks when a mysterious, giant object came floating slowly toward them. They seemed happy to see Captain Gray, little knowing what was later to befall them as a result of their contact with Europeans.

Here the salmon begin their inland journey up the Columbia. In the last century these salmon could swim either to the base of the Columbia Mountains, two hundred miles into Canada, or to Red Fish Lake nine hundred miles away in Idaho. A few probably made it as far as Nevada. They can't do so now with over 130 dams blocking this great river and its tributaries.

The Columbia River once supported the largest Chinook runs in the world. Historically, 10 to 16 million salmon came up the river each year. By 1980 the run was down to 4 to 5 million. By the mid-1980s runs had dropped to 2 to 2.5 million, of which only 300 to 500 thousand were wild fish. In 1991 when only one female sockeye returned to Red Fish Lake to spawn, the National Marine Fisheries Service officially declared the Snake River sockeye to be an endangered species. In April 1992 the Snake River spring, summer and fall Chinook were listed as threatened species.

The white settlers quickly appreciated the richness of these salmon runs and the first Columbia River cannery was built in 1867. By 1880 Columbia River canneries were packing over 25 million pounds of salmon a year. New and more efficient techniques, such as the fish wheel,

Hundreds of dams block the passage of salmon up the streams in the Pacific Northwest with disastrous consequences to the salmon populations. Attempts to move fish around these dams are expensive and often ineffective. These dams, combined with massive degradation of the streamside environment, have severely reduced salmon and steelhead populations.

were introduced. The fish wheel turned with the current, catching salmon with each revolution. By 1900 seventy-nine fish-wheels were operating round the clock on the Columbia, mining this resource almost to extinction.

The lucky survivors encountered new problems. The forests were being harvested to provide lumber and other wood products for the rapidly growing population. Salmon need to spawn in gravel, and the eggs require cool water. Silt from deforested slopes soon covers the gravel in the streambed. Unprotected by the forest canopy, the water heats up and the eggs and fry die.

Overharvesting and habitat destruction soon devastated the natural runs, and fish hatcheries were built to restore them. The first Northwest hatchery was built in 1877 on the Clackamas River near Portland.

Then came the dams. Bonneville, the first federal dam on the Columbia, forty miles east of Portland, continued the decline of the wild salmon runs. The dam was begun in 1933 and provided jobs for three thousand workers in the midst of the Depression. When it was finished in 1938, it backed up the Columbia River for forty-eight miles. Once the dam was completed, the giant chinook salmon, called June hogs for their weight of 125 pounds, kept ramming their heads against the concrete. They couldn't seem to find the fish ladders built on both sides of the dam.

Fifty miles upstream, water from The Dalles Dam covers Celilo Falls where the local natives once speared migrating fish. And so on, one dam after another, 136 of them. Fish can pass by certain dams but not others. They can't pass over Grand Coulee, which blocks their runs in over a thousand miles of streams in northeast Washington, northern Montana and most of the original runs in Canada. The Hell's Canyon Dam ended the great runs to the dry lands of southern Idaho. The Chandler Dam on the Yakima River, built without a fish ladder, wiped out a sockeye run that sometimes numbered six hundred thousand fish a year.

On a flight to Portland, I happen to sit next to Roy Webster, onetime executive vice president for the Pacific Northwest Waterways Association. He is a great enthusiast of the Columbia River dams, reservoirs and waterways. He ticks off some of their achievements: low-cost transportation—barges can go all the way from Astoria at the mouth of the Columbia to Lewiston on the Idaho border; low-cost energy—the Columbia River hydroelectric dams produce one-third of the hydroelectric power in the United States. Just after World War II, before the upstream dams were built, a heavy spring rain and snowmelt wiped out Vanport, a city of forty thousand on the Oregon shore north of Portland. The dams mean better flood control, irrigation, navigation and recreation. Over ten billion dollars worth of goods are carried up and down the river. The waters irrigate twenty-five million acres.

The dams impede or block the salmon's upward journey to their spawning grounds, but they may wreak an even greater destruction when the smolts migrate downstream. It is estimated that between sixty and ninety percent of juvenile chinook and sockeye are killed as they pass through the large, slow waters impounded by dams on the Columbia or in the turbines themselves. The dams create slackwater pools that slow the fish's migration. Their seaward journey has been extended from one to six weeks, increasing their exposure to predators and other conditions that kill them and make them vulnerable to stress and disease.

By 1980 it was apparent to everyone that wild salmon were in serious trouble, and Congress enacted the Pacific Northwest Electric Power Planning and Conservation Act. Fish were given equal status with power, irrigation and forestry. The Act created the Northwest Power Planning Council (NPPC), which has the responsibility of preparing a program to protect fish and wildlife affected by hydroelectric projects on the Columbia River. One major goal is to increase the return of fish to the mouth of the Columbia River by five million a year. To do so, the NPPC has developed broad, expensive and, hopefully, effective strategies to help overcome many of the problems that have contributed to the fish's decline.

A major part of the plan is to make it easier for the young salmon to get safely to sea. Hundreds of thousands of smolts, mostly hatchery stock but also many wild ones, are barged down the river. Biologists worry about how well these smolts pick up the necessary cues for returning while taking a leisurely boat trip to the ocean. The NPPC has also been trying to flush the young salmon downstream. This is done by releasing water from the dam, which increases the flow of the river.

The downside of this plan is that it also reduces the amount of stored water needed later in the year for irrigation and power generation. When this salmon-friendly strategy was tried on two dams on the Snake River, its impact hit home. The salmon were able to get through more easily, but hydroelectric power was reduced by a dramatic forty percent, barge shipping was halted, and irrigation pumps were left high and dry.

Hatcheries will continue to produce the bulk of fish. On the Columbia River over 100 hatcheries produce 170 to 200 million smolts. Many biologists worry about the impact of these hatchery-bred fish on wild populations, however, since wild salmon and steelhead are finely adapted to their environment. For example, on one Canadian stream one group of sockeye stock spawn in a tributary to the lake feeding the stream. Their fry are adapted to swim downstream to the lake. Another stock spawns below the lake and their fry are adapted to swim upstream into the lake. A third stock spawns in a creek just below the lake outlet stream. Its fry swim into the outlet stream and then up into the lake. Each of these three stocks have slightly different behaviors, and each adaptation might allow the species to survive in adverse conditions. Hatchery fish, which come from a small genetic stock, are often unsuccessful living in the wild, perhaps because they lack this fine-tuned genetic wisdom. Some hatchery fish mate with wild fish and the result may be a reduction in the wild fish's adaptability. Despite years of trying, hatcheries have not been able to increase wild salmon numbers.

There are other problems with hatchery fish. Large hatchery fish eat wild juvenile salmon, and all hatchery fish compete for food and space. Hatchery fish mate as aggressively as wild fish but often lack subtle behavioral characteristics developed to create social dominance at minimal expense of energy. Having overcome innumerable waterfalls, rocks, predators and other obstructions, a tired wild fish can ill afford to bash heads repeatedly with an ill-tempered hatchery competitor who doesn't know when it is time to give up.

Nancy Simmerman

Tom & Pat Leeson

Anglers complain of ever-diminishing runs in many rivers. In the coastal streams and rivers of Oregon, wild coho salmon are down to an all-time low. In 1991 the American Fisheries Society identified 101 stocks of salmon at high risk of extinction, 58 at moderate risk of extinction, and 54 stocks of special concern, most in the Northwest. The survey found that 106 additional stocks are already extinct. A new Wilderness Society report says nine out of ten salmon species in Idaho, Oregon, Washington and California are extinct or at risk of extinction—coho; spring, summer and fall Chinook; chum; summer- and winter-run steelhead; and sockeye. Overall, forty percent of the salmon stocks are extinct in their historical range, thirteen percent are endangered, fourteen percent threatened, and seventeen percent of special concern. Only sixteen percent appear robust.

Kathleen Norris Cook

R. Valentine Atkinson

It may seem inconsistent that I plead for the salvation of salmon, when I am willing to catch some myself. I always prefer to release any fish I catch—and I would never keep a wild (endangered) salmon in the lower forty-eight states. If the salmon or steelhead runs are healthy, however, I think recreational fishermen should keep a few fish if they want.

Many people catch fish to eat—the fish are a healthy source of food—and eating them also keeps one connected to the stream, the great outdoors and the salmon.

We are better off allowing wild fish to spawn in their natural habitat and ensuring that those habitats are protected or restored. Imagine a salmon entering the tributaries of a stream like Catherine Creek, a tributary to the Grande Ronde that eventually enters the Columbia. Even fifty years ago the salmon could find protection in a number of deep pools under logs and overhanging trees. Today only twenty-five percent of such pools remain. The salmon that are left swim much more exposed to the land and sky. The stream has been simplified, stream channels have been straightened, and the banks stripped of trees. Logjams, slides and root balls have been removed, making the stream much more vulnerable to erosion, drought and floods. In a big storm silt from the eroded banks can choke off a stream.

If the Bonneville Power Authority wishes to reduce hydroelectric production to help the salmon, alternate energy sources must be developed to satisfy the increasing energy needs of the West Coast. But what would these sources be? Nuclear energy? Coal? This seems an odd environmental trade-off—smolts for volts—and the costs are enormous. The Bonneville Power Authority estimates that it has already spent one billion dollars for the survival of the salmon, mostly through lost power-generation revenues.

I have heard about the winter salmon and steelhead runs in the Cowlitz River in Washington and decide to give them a try in December when the steelhead run is the best. These are mostly hatchery fish, easily identified because a useless tail fin has been removed to mark them from wild fish. Some friends have requested a fish for a special party they are planning in Portland, and I am willing to oblige them.

On the day I plan to go fishing I am scheduled to meet Dawhna, my guide from Clancy's Guide Service, at 5:30 a.m. at Spiffy's restaurant, ten miles south of Chehalis in southeastern Washington. The human energy and excitement at Spiffy's this early in the morning is alarming—the place is packed with fishermen. At 6:00 we leave to get in line for the river launch at Blue Creek. There are plenty of hearty fishermen and a few fisherwomen who want to catch one of these big, bright fish. One by one, the power boats drift off into the early morning light and my turn soon comes.

The Cowlitz is a big stream that flows along thickly forested banks. We use very light eleven-foot graphite rods with spinning reels. Dawhna has attached a swivel to the end of the line, hangs a weight from one end of the swivel, and ties on a three-foot leader with a red hook at the end. She shows me how to thread a glob of salmon eggs onto the hook and tie it down with a loop from the line. Then we drift on down, soon passing a line of seventy-five or so bank anglers casting shoulder-to-shoulder in the deep hole where Blue Creek flows into the Cowlitz. Several of these lucky anglers already have fish on. This first hour of fishing is supposed to be the best for steelhead and I am strike happy. At first I strike at every little nibble, often jerking off the roe until I get a feel for the sinker bouncing on the bottom. Dawhna is also fishing since there are only two of us in the boat. She misses a strike.

First, we fish in the big hole below Blue Creek—presumably the steelhead are stacked up here. The drift is thick with boats that motor up to the top of the run, then drift back down to the bottom. We watch a few boats pick up some nice steelhead. Then Dawhna decides to go on downstream. We cast next to the shore. Dawhna has told me to be careful not to pull too hard on what may feel like a snag because it might be a fish. Sometimes the fish will also swim upstream and the line will actually go slack.

Then I get one. It happens so fast—not a strong grab, but a sudden, firm pulling at the end of my line. Steelhead will mouth the bait, sucking it in and quickly spitting it out. I am accustomed to catching smaller fish, easy to reel in; but this is a strong fish and I need to pull it in carefully, lifting my rod, then quickly reeling down. After a struggle, Dawhna nets my fish, which weighs eight pounds and puts it in the fish box.

Around ten o'clock the sun comes out briefly, but the air gets colder. This is a beautiful place to fish. The fishermen are friendly, waving and smiling as they roar by in their boats. Some sing to Dawhna, "Oh, Donna. Oh, Donna." We drift on down, fishing the shore in the pleasant rhythm of the stream. We try to keep our bait in the water on the bottom, using every minute of the drift. When I break off the line, which happens often, Dawhna whips another one on. We lose little fishing time.

A female bald eagle rises from the limbs of a cottonwood tree and soars over the river looking for fish. I am thrilled and reassured by the presence of this magnificent fellow fisher. The bald eagle may someday come back in such numbers as to be commonplace—I hope so—but it is still a rare treat for me to see one. Seeing her rivets me to this time and place, assuring me that I will always remember my experience here.

At about one o'clock I decide to stop fishing—I have finally caught one of these magical creatures! I feel like Rudyard Kipling when he caught his first Columbia River chinook:

I have lived! The American continent may now sink under the sea, for I have taken the best it yields and the best was neither dollars nor love nor real estate.

Then a problem arises. When I call my friends in Portland, they have decided to cook something else for dinner. I have this fish in my trunk that cannot be wasted. I buy enough ice to keep it fresh for a few hours and decide to drive to the Indian reservation near The Dalles Dam. After I check in at the reservation hotel, I offer my fish to the young clerk and her family, who accept it with delight.

On my drive back to Portland from The Dalles, a rainbow emerges from the clouds. It seems to arise from the Columbia Gorge itself, connecting the river to the sky, shimmering against the wet, brown mountains. I see this as a sign of hope, of resurrection. Congress has mandated that the fish must survive. The governor of Idaho is calling for a "Salmon Czar" who will have the authority to save the salmon. The governor persists in this effort, even though his home constituency offers him strong opposition. There are even bold plans to build a fish canal around the dams—for an estimated cost of six billion dollars. This expensive solution will probably never happen, but that it is even being considered demonstrates how committed many people are to these fish.

Of course, all the landside efforts will be meaningless if the fish are not protected at sea. What I said before still applies: Commercial harvests need to be cut down, drift net fishing ended, and seaside predators controlled.

Berry Peril

There are so many beautiful coastal streams. My favorite is the Smith River, the last free-running stream in Northern California. A drive along this river will soften the soul. Catching a fish in it will change your life—or so I imagine. In January, on a sunny day near the Oregon border on the Middle Fork of the Smith, I hiked down a steep slope through a thick forest. The river was still many feet below me, running through granite rocks that created deep green pools and waterfalls. Great fish moved silently through these pools, or maybe they were still resting, exhausted from coming up the falls. No other people were in sight—all the sounds were of river and birds.

The Endangered Species Act is a powerful weapon to help preserve a threatened or endangered population. If a species qualifies, extreme measures can be taken for its preservation. In coming years the genetics, environment and behavior of the fish in many of these rivers will be studied, and, presumably, many of the fish will be classified as threatened or endangered. If so, they can be protected and their preservation will involve restoration and preservation of many streams, mountains and forests. If enacted, a proposed protection plan would result in less logging, livestock grazing and recreation along thousands of miles of streams but only on lands east of the Cascade Range. This effort may not be enough, but it is certainly a move in the right direction.

Kathleen Norris Cook

R. Valentine Atkinson

R. Valentine Atkinson

Tom Montgomery

David Stoecklein

They say that there are five stages in a fly fisherman's life. First to catch a fish on a fly, then to catch a lot of small fish, then to catch a big fish, then to catch a lot of big fish, then to catch a wild winter steelhead. I decided it was time to pursue the latter. Having read about the famous Vancouver Island streams, like the Nimpkish, Salmon, Campbell and Gold, and curious about what was happening to salmon and steelhead runs in these streams, I headed one March for the town of Campbell River on the west shore of Vancouver Island. Roderick Haig-Brown made this region famous with books like *Fisherman's Summer, Return to the River* and *A River Never Sleeps.* In the latter he writes:

> *A river is water in its loveliest form; rivers have life and sound and movement and infinity of variation, rivers are veins of the earth through which the life blood returns to the heart.*

Describing what it is like to know a river, he says lovingly of the Campbell:

> *…one learns to hope for the sight of a pileated woodpecker crossing the river in swooping flight at this place, a flock of mergansers at that place, a dipper against black rocks and rippled water somewhere else, deer coming down to eat the moss on the rocks on the water's edge in hard weather. All these things are precious in repetition and, repeated or no, they build the river for one. They are part of the background of knowing and loving it, as is every fish hooked, every cast fished through, every rock trodden. And men and women come strongly into it. Here, I remind myself, was where Ann sat that first day we came up the river together. …*

I will not have time to know the rivers so well on this first trip, but I am looking forward to meeting them.

In the summer the Campbell area is packed with people fishing for salmon in the ocean and streams, but the winter sees only a few solitary fishermen in pursuit of winter steelhead.

Chris Barker, my guide for the weekend, has been fishing in the Campbell River area ever since he first read Haig-Brown's books in his youth. He decides we will fish the Gold, which lies on the other side of the island. Just out of Campbell River, we enter Strathcona Provincial Park. I am shocked to see that large sections of the mountain slopes in the park have been clear-cut. Chris tells me that the logging occurred years before the region became a park. The damage is even more painful because the trees have been so slow to recover. What must the rest of the island be like where the timber is not protected and the logging continues mostly unabated?

It is snowing heavily at the pass and I worry that the west side of the island will be socked in. I know what Chris is thinking: "Perfect steelhead conditions." I imagine myself in a stream with two inches of snow on my hat. In Gold River, a little logging town whose existence is threatened by the planned closure of its pulp and paper mill, four fishermen from Washington state are waiting for the restaurant to open in this seemingly deserted community. They are wearing T-shirts over their winter clothing that say "12% not 21%." I ask them what this means. They say they are not sure, but that they just like the color. Later I learn that this slogan refers to a recently released government report recommending protection of 21 percent of the forests. The loggers only want 12 percent to be so designated—which means that 88 percent of the land could be stripped of trees. One reason the town is so deserted is that a convoy of loggers has headed south to Victoria, the provincial capital, for a massive rally planned to oppose restrictions on cutting timber. I feel sorry for the loggers and their families who might lose income if the proposals are adopted, but a change in this lifestyle is inevitable someday since there are a finite number of trees.

Meanwhile, the weather warms slightly and the snow turns to rain as we leave for the river. We try a few places upstream with no success. Then after lunch we move down to the bottom of the Gold River. On the left side, at the mouth of the river where it enters Muchalat Inlet, there are twenty or so wooden frame buildings, most in disrepair, home to the ancestors of the Muchalat Indian Tribe. On the other side of the road, also on the bay, a ponderous paper and pulp factory sends billows of white smoke tainted with a chlorine smell to join the rain clouds. The water in front of the mill is filled with logs ready to be processed. This mill may have to be shut down, since it can no longer compete with cheaper products imported from South America, but it will leave its legacy on the surrounding countryside. Chris tells me that chemicals from the plant have begun to leach into the stream. The juxtaposition of a huge, ugly mill tucked at the end of a peaceful, deep blue bay next to a golden river seasonally flushed with fish is painful to me. I am distressed because of the irrevocable damage it has done to the landscape and because of the realization that many people will lose jobs when it closes. Ironically, this mill or ones like it have produced the paper I so depend upon and use with abandon.

We drive back to the head of a trail hidden in the brush. As we climb down from the roadway, we are soon surrounded by old-growth timber—some of the trees are a hundred feet tall—and my mind is cleared of gloomy thoughts. The tangled roots of the trees are covered with bright green moss. Shiny stones churned up from the river bottom are wedged in the roots, creating a mosaic of wood, moss and stone. The trees are thick enough to protect us from the drizzle until Chris leads me out to the middle of the river. There I begin casting toward the edge of a faster current. The water is very clear and very cold. Chris worries that the steelhead will be in the deeper holes, hard to reach with a fly; and if they aren't, that they will be reluctant to bite. After about ten casts, my fly line stops. I see the gray-green back of a big fish move perpendicular to the flow and shoot downstream, my hook firmly in place. The line is rapidly stripped from my reel as the steelhead continues to run. The tippet at the end of my line was designed for a fish weighing less than six pounds and Chris says this fish is probably fifteen pounds or more. If I try to stop it by increasing the drag on the line, the tippet will break. For me, it is not a question of bringing in the fish, but of how long I can fight it. The steelhead pulls out the hundred feet of my green polyester line and goes into the white dacron backing. Except for a few pauses, it moves relentlessly to the safety of the sea. I am not able to move downstream after it because the bottom is too rocky and treacherous, so I wait helplessly. I will have to stop the fish before the line reaches the end of the spool or take a chance of losing my whole line. Then I feel a snap as the line breaks or the hook comes out. The steelhead is gone. Did having that fish on my line count? Have I reached the fifth stage of a fisherman's life? Did I catch a wild steelhead? No, I only hooked one. To qualify, I would need to release the fly myself, my fingers touching the hard mouth of the fish. Yet I am exhilarated to have felt the power of that steelhead, its every move transmitted directly to my senses. I am happy to have hooked the fish, but it has all seemed so improbable.

R. Valentine Atkinson

Tom Montgomery

R. Valentine Atkinson

As one who fishes on many different streams, I have come to rely on guides to take me to the right spots and show me what to do. I can explore and discover the river on my own later, but first I want to catch a fish. Of the many guides I have followed, the ones who stand out seem to love the rivers they fish, be determined to help me catch a fish, and want to create a pleasant day.

Tom & Pat Leeson

Willard Clay

Clear-cuts rip the soul from the forest, leaving ugly, deformed, gaping holes. They do much more than scar the surface, however. The tangled mass left behind becomes a dangerous crossing for forest animals. The stripped soil holds water poorly and rain causes deep erosion, washing down silt that chokes and muddies the rivers below.

R. Valentine Atkinson

Bald eagles add spice to a wilderness experience and often congregate where salmon spawn. These magnificent birds have a wingspan that reaches six feet and eyes that can see a rabbit from two miles away. They mate for life, may live thirty years or more and build huge nests that can weigh as much as two tons. Bald eagles have always been plentiful in Alaska and Canada but have become seriously threatened in the lower forty-eight states. At one time there were fifty thousand bald eagles in the continental United States. By 1972, mainly because of hunting, lost habitat and the pesticide DDT that caused the eagles to lay thin-shelled eggs that broke before hatching, there were only eight hundred breeding pairs. Protected by the Endangered Species Act of 1973, bald eagles have slowly recovered and there are now over three thousand breeding pairs.

The next day it rains steadily. Chris is excited because the rain will muddy the water, and the fish will become more brazen and accessible, less able to inspect the fly before taking it. Maybe even more fish will move into the river as it rises. There is a price to pay, however: I must now wade through deeper and swifter water to get to my casting spot. By noon the water is up to my crotch and I am worried. Chris tells me to keep an eye on the river because it can come up real fast. Later when I talk with Kevin, another long-time guide, he tells me that the water can rise four feet in an hour because the slopes around the stream have been stripped, and the water drains straight into it.

When I wade downriver, trying to cast my fly into the water where the fish lie, each footstep becomes harder and less certain. I look anxiously at the safe shore sixty feet away across the rising stream. Finally, I decide to break for lunch, dreading the walk back to shore. Sometimes, when I step forward, the current carries my foot farther down than I had intended and I almost fall backward. I remember the many times I have slipped and fallen into rivers and my fear mounts. At the least I would get wet and miserable, and I could drown.

At lunch Chris tells me a harrowing story of a near-drowning. He had been fishing with his twelve-year-old son and the boy had walked out onto a logjam. When his son stepped onto one of the logs, it gave way and he fell into the stream. He was immediately washed under the logs. When Chris saw him go under, he realized that his son's only possible escape would be to swim up against a current greater than his strength. In a flash Chris dove into the river, found his son struggling under the log-jam, grabbed him and came back upstream, pulling the boy to safety. The son was shaken and chastened but otherwise all right.

After lunch, with this tale in mind and the rain pouring down, I go back to the stream. To fend off the cold, I put on another pair of socks and another pair of pants under my waders. The first step into the stream is the worst, but nothing compared to the feeling when the water comes up over my waist. When that happens, I always gasp and feel a moment of suffocation. Once I have warmed up and begun anticipating my excellent chances of catching a fish, however, my fear disappears into the rhythmic casting. Why? I am not sure. Was I reassured by Chris's act of heroism—not likely. Chris has waded to shore and climbed a tree to see if he can spot some fish from a higher point. He would never have time to reach me if I fell in. Perhaps warming up gives me a feeling of greater strength. I have also convinced myself that I could swim to safety if I went under.

I begin to experience fish illusions. I am looking for a shadow moving in front of the lighter rocks, a shape changing against the ever-changing pattern of the waves. Each time I think I spot a fish, it becomes, upon deeper scrutiny, a rock or the shadow of a rock. When I look at the shore, the pattern of the waters is momentarily imposed on the trees, which seem to move like flowing water.

By late afternoon my arm is tired, and I decide this will be a fishless day.

That evening in a local cafe I have dinner with Kevin, who is taking two customers

There are many great salmon and steelhead streams on the southern British Columbia coast. The three most famous are the Fraser, Dean and Skeena Rivers. The Dean has seen a slow decline in the number of steelhead since 1984, although the numbers remain higher than they were in the seventies. The overall wild steelhead catch estimated for British Columbia has declined from a high of around 120 thousand fish in 1988-89 to about 70 thousand a few years later. Although the outlook for steelhead is depressing, some rivers, such as the Somass system, seem to be having an increased return.

over to the Gold tomorrow. Kevin describes days in other years of catching and releasing fifty fish on lures on the Gold. He wonders aloud why I am willing to spend eight hours in a cold river in the rain and be so happy to hook one fish that I have virtually no chance of landing.

Maybe I like being on the edge, I explain—on the edge of the stream, the river just high enough to bring the fish up from the deeper holes to a rift where I can reach them, but not too high that I can't wade out. I like the immediate, intense connection between the fish and me that a fly line and the supple fly rod provide, and the electricity of the strike. I only use lures when fly-fishing is impossible. It might seem a little peculiar to pay good money to have someone stand in a tree and watch me whip a nine-foot graphite stick back and forth in the middle of a cold stream, with better chances of catching a cold than a fish. But there was a fish there, I say, and yes, it was worth it.

The chances of catching a winter steelhead are worse now than they have been in years. Both Chris and Kevin are worried about the salmon and steelhead runs in British Columbia—and they should be. The current winter runs are only about fifty to sixty percent of the potential. There are only about seven thousand summer steelhead and about four times as many winter ones. The original winter steelhead in the Campbell River are probably extinct, as are the sea-run cutthroat trout that came up in great numbers until the seventies. The steelhead are particularly vulnerable to stream conditions because they spend the first several years of their life in fresh water. The British Columbia salmon and steelhead populations face the same problems as other Pacific Coast fish but with a local twist. There has been severe degradation of the habitat in this area; too much commercial fishing; and, in the last few years, a few bad breaks from mother nature, including strong winter floods that washed

out the spawning grounds and a summer drought that killed off many of the young fish. Then there is *El Niño*, a warm current resulting from a change in the normal weather pattern of the Pacific Ocean. *El Niño* has raised the temperature of the Pacific Northwest waters while reducing their nutrients.

Hungry, hot salmon have headed north, and *El Niño* has brought an untold number of mackerel, normally a warm-water fish, to the British Columbia coast. These mackerel decimate the young salmon as they enter the ocean at the rivers' mouths. Kevin says he has even seen mackerel swimming up into the streams.

The clear-cutting of the trees has also had an impact on the streams and the salmon and will continue to do so for another century. Kevin notes that the Gold used to be crystal clear. Now it turns brown and murky during a heavy rainfall. He can describe different types of damage to almost all of the streams he fishes. Of the ninety primary watersheds on the island, only eight remain mostly unaffected.

British Columbia has over thirty-nine hundred streams and rivers that support salmon populations, some of them huge. Haig-Brown claimed that over eighteen million salmon came back in the late fifties to just one branch of the Fraser River that runs through the city of Vancouver and drains much of the interior plateau of British Columbia. The status of these salmon stocks is not clear. Seventy-six percent of the salmon stocks are considered stable or increasing, and twenty-four percent are declining. In 1991 over forty-three hundred commercial vessels harvested over eighty thousand tons of salmon in British Columbian waters, about nine percent of the world's supply of commercially caught salmon.

The economy of British Columbia is so heavily tied to logging—an estimated twelve percent of the economy depends directly upon it—that the logging companies command political clout. These loggers want the timber. Local environmentalists believe that only international pressure will succeed in stopping the clear-cutting.

Pondering such issues, I turn again to the writings of Haig-Brown, whose house is only two doors down from where I am staying. Chris tells me I am welcome to stop by and visit it, I just have to notify the caretaker first. The wooden, shingled house sits on the Campbell River next to a little park and a creek. An overgrown pink camellia bush obscures the right side of the steps leading up to the front door. I am looking for some feeling, looking for a sign of hope. I enter his library where he wrote his books. Thousands of volumes cover the walls. I read from *A River Never Sleeps:*

> *I still don't know why I fish or why other men fish, except that we like it and it makes us think and feel. But I do know that if it were not for the strong, quick life of rivers, for the sparkle in the sunshine, for the cold grayness of them under rain and the feel of them about my legs as I set my feet hard down on rocks or sand or gravel, I should fish less often. …Perhaps fishing is, for me, only an excuse to be near rivers.*

I realize there may be an even better way to pay homage to this great man. I put on my waders and walk to the very places he so often fished. Even at twilight, with minutes of daylight left, there is a chance of some great fish lying in the stream, ready to take my fly.

WHERE WILD RIVERS RUN

SOMETHING HAPPENED IN 1988 THAT CHANGED my relationship with salmon and led to my obsession with this book: I had an opportunity to experience them in their almost natural state on the Situk River near Yakutat, Alaska. In April of that year, my brother called to say that he was sending me an application for a fishing lottery. If I were selected, I would get to stay in a Forest Service cabin on the Situk River in late August, the time of one of the best silver salmon runs in the world. Silver salmon are particularly desired by salmon fly fishermen because they readily take a fly and fight with great strength, determination and acrobatics. They are also delicious. I sent in my form along with, I suppose, several thousand other hopeful fishermen. I was astounded when, about a month later, I learned that I had won a slot.

On the day of the trip, we flew to Yakutat, 150 miles northwest of Juneau, up the Inland Passage along the vast snow-capped mountains that rise straight up from the deep green sea. Long turquoise glaciers are cutting deep valleys in these ranges as they slide slowly down to the ocean. The glacier surfaces are streaked with brown from rock and snow slides. The broad, irregular patterns of sea and mountains are broken only occasionally by the bright white specks of ships far below, or a town or port cut at the edge of the forest. Until you see the rectangular clear-cut plots gouged out of the virgin forests, the land seems unharmed by humankind. These plots are particularly ugly on the Tongass National Forest, which surrounds Situk. There the natural forest meets a rectangular meadow of stumps. The dark green velvet texture of the trees is juxtaposed against soggy ocher. Dramatic contrasts of color, shape and form in nature can be wonderful: the edge where land meets ocean, strata from an ancient seabed thrust up mountain high, a spiderweb in bougainvillea. Even humanmade ones can be lovely, such as the Golden Gate Bridge or the Great Wall of China as seen from a satellite. In this forest, however, the contrast between trees and no trees foretells the end of wilderness.

After landing we mill around the airfield waiting to be flown to the cabin. The bush pilots all look like escaped convicts with a hangover. When our turn comes, the pilot crams our food and gear into the plane and we take off. The cabin is only eight miles from town and I am just settling into the flight when we start to land. The plane hits the runway as soon as we pass over the river and rolls to a terrifying stop, jarring back and forth on the grassy uneven surface. A woman and her child appear out of the woods to greet the plane. She introduces herself as Jane and says she has been hired by the Forest Service to mow the grass on the landing strip and has been living in our end of the cabin with her husband and two children. Jane seems annoyed that she will have to move out to make room for us. She has big biceps covered with indecipherable tattoos and speaks with a deep voice. I hope she doesn't get too annoyed.

Cabin? Actually, the cabin is an A-frame divided in the middle into two sections. Half of the wall to the south is covered with Plexiglas, which lets in light, but very little, so the inside is dim. There is a propane stove for heat, one door and no windows. The place is damp.

Jane and her family carry their stuff out to a lawn-sized clearing framed by poles used by hunters to hang their meat. Then she thinks better of these accommodations and asks the pilot to return for them later since she will finish her mowing by the end of the day. The only messages that leave here must be taken out by word-of-mouth since there is no telephone, radio or transmitter.

I am very surprised by this Alaska. Although I once took a cruise ship up the Inland Passage, and have read many articles and books about it and seen my share of Alaskan nature movies, I am shocked at how dense the foliage is around the cabin and the stream. I can't go twenty feet without disappearing into the dark forest. The cabin sits on the bank of the Yakutak River, which is now about twenty feet across. Only the ground immediately around the cabin, the landing strip and parts of the riverbank are clear. A trail has been cut downstream for a hundred feet or so, and upstream to the edge of the river. There is also a trail leading straight up a logging road about two miles away. In fact, we can hear the sound of chain saws, and about half an hour later two young men emerge from a trail that opens onto the runway. They say that they have been hired by the Forest Service to cut back the foliage along this trail in case anyone needs to use it. When they leave, I can see a little cut indicating a trail head. Four days later this trail has disappeared. I feel claustrophobic in Alaska. The forest is a dense tangle of trees, brambles, bushes and ferns. I am sure bears are lurking somewhere.

Ironically, we find that the best traveling routes are bear trails (more like bear tunnels). We walk nervously along these trails, heads bowed to avoid the brush above us, talking loudly to

All the major rivers in Alaska run free and many of these are flush with salmon. In the Yukon, however, the chum numbers are way down, perhaps because of

scare the bears and stepping on bear scat dimpled with the remains of berries and bones.

An hour later our companions, Rich and Jim, arrive on the next flight. By this time my brother Brooke and I are already fishing by the cabin. They join us and we walk upstream along the bank. The river seems very quiet, but as we get closer, we can see movement in the water—salmon. Rich is using a spinning rod with a lure and immediately catches a small Dolly Varden. I try a chartreuse fly that my friend Alex has tied for me. I cast into the water, not knowing what to expect. When nothing happens in that spot, I move upstream. In a moment I feel a strong strike from a fairly large fish and catch my first pink, a.k.a. humpback salmon, so-named because of the large hump that develops on its back during its upward migration. The fish is strong, but I have little trouble bringing him in. His silver sheen has started to turn red and green, his upper jaw has begun to curve over his lower, and his lower jaw has developed two sharp teeth. The fly is lodged in his lower jaw. I remove it and release the fish. He shoots off into the deeper water. This is the first of many humpies I will catch.

We hope to catch silver salmon, also called coho, because they are bigger and better fighters than the humpies. The silver salmon wait at the mouth of the Yakutak, then move up the river in groups of a thousand or more fish. They make the eight-mile journey to the spawning lake in a day or two unless they stop in one of the deeper pools along the way. We spend a pleasant afternoon catching humpies, Dolly Varden and a few rainbows. Here there are no motors, no telephones, no radios, no televisions and only an occasional bush plane flying overhead. Most of the noise is talk.

overfishing in the Bering Sea. Every run must always be considered fragile. Vast stretches of Alaska are being clear-cut and some rivers mined for gold.

As a kid, I loved to sit around the camp fire and tell ghost stories. In Alaska you sit around the camp fire and tell bear stories. When we arrive back at the cabin, Frank Jones and his uncle, who have drawn the north end of the cabin, are frying steaks in a pan over an open fire. About the second word out of Frank's mouth is the beginning of a long stream of bear stories (and plane crash stories, gun stories and Alaskan women stories). Bear stories make the wilderness more delicious.

"You see this gun," Frank says as he pulls his .457 Kazul out of the holster strapped to his belt. "I carry this gun because it is the only handgun that can stop a bear. Let me show you." He aims his gun at a nearby tree and fires. The bullet goes right through the tree.

"I got that sucker," he says, laughing.

We shoot trees. The loud bang of the gun is quickly absorbed in the deep forest around us.

Later we drink wine and beer. There are few night sounds—not even birds, although an occasional goose or duck flies by. We hear splashing in the river as some big salmon breaks the surface or makes a place to mate.

By ten o'clock the evening light has finally begun to fade.

Feeling chilly, we move inside. The propane stove is lit through some inscrutable process that requires an hour of experimentation before it fires up. We have plenty of food, as each of us has brought enough to last for two weeks. We fry the Dolly Varden in a pan with butter and bacon, foods we normally consider poisonous, and drink more wine. Then we retire to bed, encountering the uneasy sleep of an unknown place. I listen for the sounds of a great grizzly tearing through the Plexiglas.

We wake early, boil intense coffee and cook pancakes spotted with blueberries we pick from the omnipresent bushes. Then we head upstream along the river, looking for good fishing spots. Whenever the brush comes right up against the water and the stream is too deep to cross, we must find our way around. Even these little diversions from our path can be exhausting. As we fight our way through the dense brush, our fly lines keep coming off and tangling on branches. It takes us half an hour to walk a few hundred feet upstream.

After we have each settled into our spot, I have what I have thought of ever since as the salmon experience. I am fishing in a spot where the water is shallow and I can see the riverbed maybe five feet down. I am casting upstream with a leader designed to sink right to the bottom. As soon as my fly touches the bed of the river and is pulled across it by the current, a humpie strikes. Then the numbers of fish begin to increase so that a trickle of one or two becomes a constant stream. I can see them coming over a little waterfall, racing into the hole where I am fishing and then disappearing upstream. The color of the water changes with the coming fish as their red sides mix with the surface of the river. They become one with the water, reflections on reflections, making patterns with the water. Losing focus, I merge with the fish. I stop fishing and just stare at the river. Its surface changes with the wind, sometimes only catching the reflection of the sky, then shifting suddenly to reveal the great movement beneath. I see the red blood cells flowing in my veins, the stream within the stream, the vast assemblage of these determined beasts. The life in the river.

And that is it. A brief moment. When I look up, the world has not changed. I feel the same passion to catch the fish, but now I feel differently about the salmon, and I still do. I feel that we must not lose this magnificent event, the spawning of the salmon, and that many others must see it. Maybe I am just being selfish, but I want this to be part of my future, and my daughter's future.

Brooke has a topo map that shows a big pool about a mile up the stream from our cabin, and he and I decide to walk up to it to see if some big salmon have schooled up. We start out following what seems to be a bear trail leading in the right direction but it soon dissolves into suggestions of paths. Before we know it, we have wandered away from the side of the stream. Though we are no more than a few hundred feet from the cabin, we are lost. We keep pushing through the undergrowth in hopes of coming across the stream, but progress is very difficult. We can't see over the bush, and we can't see through it. We also must slog through the occasional marsh that crosses our path. I am in poor physical shape and soon tire as I walk along in my bulky waders. Branches sting my eyes and I slip on the wet ground. When we reach the side of the stream nearly an hour later, we find that we are at almost the same spot where we started fishing yesterday.

R. Valentine Atkinson

Grizzly bears may weigh half a ton and look as big as a Volkswagen Beetle but you can't outrun them. The great nature writer, John McPhee, recounts the old adage that when a pine needle drops in the forest the eagle will see it fall, the deer will hear it when it hits the ground, and the bear will smell it.

Tom Mangelsen

R. Valentine Atkinson

Grizzlies are nearsighted, which is why they stand up to squint at potential foes. You are in trouble once they are down on all fours, head low, ears cocked, the hair above their hump standing on end as they start to come your way, perhaps chopping their jaws. They say that grizzlies in Alaska come running to the sound of line being stripped from a fishing reel.

Tom Montgomery

We decide to persevere and try to reach the salmon pool, this time following the bank of the river. Soon we come across a long sandbar. The sandbar is easy walking, but it is dotted with fresh bear scat; in fact, the bears might have been walking ahead of us only minutes before. The top of the sandbar is pinched off by dense foliage. We have two choices. We can either reach the hole by crossing to the other side of the river where the brush is thinner and continuing upstream; or we can hike to the end of the sandbar and enter a brush tunnel made by the bears who saunter up and down the stream.

Though only twenty feet across at this juncture, the stream seems too swift and deep for fording. But then there is the question of the bears. While I am deliberating, Brooke, who has the bear-stopping gun, has gone ahead. I have little choice if I want to proceed upstream and fish the deep salmon pool. As I walk up to the end of the sandbar where it enters the forest, I call out in a loud voice, "Here bearie, bearie, bearie. Whooo-wheee."

Entering the dark passage, I suddenly feel very alone, claustrophobic and vulnerable. I have no gun and I am not sure how far ahead Brooke is. I must walk with my head down since the bears are shorter than I am. When I emerge from the other side of the bear path, I encounter another shoreline covered with more piles of bear scat. There is no sign of Brooke. Ahead is yet another bear tunnel at the end of another sandbar. My imagination begins to run wild. What if Brooke has gone very far ahead and a bear has doubled back behind him? Then this bear would be between Brooke and me. My approach might make him feel trapped. I suspect that were I an eagle flying above me now, I would see bears just out of sight of the man exposed on the sandbar. Bush pilots say they often see a bear walking several hundred feet behind hikers, or sniffing a few hundred feet from a rafter's camp. For me, however, this danger enhances the wilderness experience. The terrain of the Lake District in England where each trail and stone has been described, if not immortalized, in verse is equally beautiful. A walk in the Scottish Highlands is exhilarating, but both of these places are less thrilling than being where real danger lurks. Unfortunately, this thrill is too great and I chicken out. Several hours later we have all reassembled back at the camp for a late lunch, a nap and preparations for the afternoon fishing.

A wind has come up and the sky fills with clouds. The temperature drops. We welcome the rain at first, assuming that it will raise the level of the water, bringing silvers into the stream. A few days later, when it has not let up, we will begin to dread it, realizing that in our wilderness isolation we are at the mercy of weather conditions. At this time of year, it could even snow. If it does, we will be stranded in the cabin until help of some sort arrives to take us out—or until we die?

After lunch we walk up along the riverbank close to the place of my Epiphany. It must have rained in the mountains already because the river has become higher and turned muddy. Fishing spots that were easy to reach before are now underwater.

Then I hear a big fish splash downstream. The rain has brought up the silvers. I see another one jump from the river. It will be long gone by the time I reach the spot where I could fish for it, but I suspect many others are coming by. I cast upriver and let my chartreuse streamer sink to the bottom before I pull it across the riverbed. The sun has just set below the tree line. The temperature goes down, but there is plenty of light to fish by. It starts to rain gently. Ten or fifteen casts later a very big and strong fish grabs my streamer and starts to race downstream. It quickly pulls out a hundred feet of line before it jumps several feet out of the water. It is a very big silver. I play him for fifteen minutes or so until he throws the hook. A few minutes later I have another one on. This fish is much smaller, so I assume it is a humpie—but when I pull it in, it is a little silver salmon. I should have kept it for eating, but I let it go, expecting that I will catch many more. I don't and the rain picks up. We realize that we will have to get off this island and cross over to the cabin side of the shore before the river becomes too deep to wade.

That night as I listen to the rain, the constant rain, I close my eyes and relive the events of the day. I expect to see the great silver salmon I almost caught, but instead I see the endless life force of the humpies—patterns of red moving relentlessly on the gravel bottom. Even now, I can close my eyes and see these fish.

I awaken in the middle of the night, needing to pee. I know there are bears close by, but where are they? I don't want to make much noise for fear of waking my mates, so I pull a raincoat over my long johns and slip quietly outside. The outhouse is too dark, cold and damp for midnight use, so I walk just far enough away from the cabin to be polite. I know bears are close. Sure enough, in the morning we see their paw marks, big as plates.

All the next day it rains and rains. A plane comes in and the fishermen on the other side of the cabin leave, to be replaced in a few hours by their friends who are using the cabin for the rest of the week. When the rain slows down—it never stops—we go after the fish, but the river has changed. The pleasant little stream has become a raging torrent. It has risen two feet and there is no longer any place that we can cross. At most spots the river is now a hundred feet wide. We walk upstream about two hundred feet to the place where we used to cross and see big fish splashing in the water.

We know the river is filled with silvers, but there are only two short stretches of shoreline we can fish from. The little stretch we were using just two hours ago is now completely underwater. I wonder if the riverbank could just overflow. I can't imagine that the Forest Service would put a cabin on the bank of a river that could flood—or would they? I start looking around for the nearest elevation. I suppose I could climb up a tree and just wait, but what would I be waiting for? Winter? Starvation? One thing is clear: walking out on the forest trail could be a real pain, if not impossible. The trail to the logging road must be underwater by now or mostly swamp.

The next morning, the day we have to leave, it is still raining. If the rain would only stop and the river go down, we would be able to catch silvers everywhere. After a few casts I hook one of these big salmon on a lure, and he pulls my line two hundred feet downstream before breaking it off. In frustration, I strip all the light line from my reel and replace it with something much stronger, but I needn't have bothered. The plane arrives to pick us up an hour early. I really don't want to leave, and I go to the pilot to complain that he has arrived too soon. Maybe he could come back later?

In a laconic, very matter-of-fact way he says, "I got some other guys to pick up. I don't know if I will be able to come back in a few hours. If you want to leave, you better do it now."

Deeply disappointed, I go find Jim and Rich and tell them that we have to go. As I do, I hear the shouts of a fisherman who has a big silver on his line. We quickly pack up our gear and fish, and load them onto the plane.

As it turns out, leaving was the right decision. Later when Alex got back to San Francisco, he called Brooke to say that it had just kept raining. Bears began prowling up and down the trail looking for dead fish, and more bears sat in the middle of the river a stone's throw away. The fishermen sat in the cabin.

R. Valentine Atkinson

I am in Anchorage on business and have two free days before I have to return to San Francisco, so I decide to explore the town. My hotel is located on a hill. If I look north, toward Elmendorf Air Force Base, I can see a river running through the city. Wondering if fish come up that stream, I walk down the hill, over the railroad tracks, past some warehouses and end up on a dirt road that leads to a boat yard. I see a number of campers parked alongside the road, and soon I come to a stream called Ship Creek. It is not very pretty. This close to the ocean, the tides come up its bed and the stream's edges are muddy tidal bottoms. It looks and smells like an estuary.

The river flows through a corrugated culvert tunnel. The entrance to the tunnel and the sides of the stream are covered with rocks. Occasionally, a fish thrashes in the water. These fish are big—twenty pounds or more—bright silver or red and fresh from the ocean. Families and friends are eating and drinking and laughing.

Fishermen sit or stand on the rocks above the culvert where the river passes under the road. Their lines all angle off the tips of their rods at about forty-five degrees from the water's surface. They have suspended globs of roe about three feet down from their Day-Glo spinners, and the whole assemblage is held on the bottom of the river by heavy lead weights. As the fish come up from the bottom, they spot these big globs of roe and spinning ornaments. Will they grab a quick snack as they pass upward, or will they simply be irritated by the whirling blades of the spinners?

A fish on his or her way to the spawning grounds usually doesn't think about food. Their stomachs are empty when they die. In spite of this, some of them grab the roe. Soon a stout fisherman jumps up and shouts that he has one on—his rod is nearly bent double. The other fishermen quickly reel in their lines. If they left them out in such close quarters, the fish would become hopelessly entangled. When the hooked salmon rolls on the surface before making a seaward run, the onlookers express their appreciation with audible gasps. These men want to keep the fish they catch for dinner—no fancy lightweight equipment designed to heighten the contest for them. They use heavy lines and heavy rods that make it easy to reel in their catch. It does not take the fisherman more than a few minutes to bring the salmon to shore. A friend wades deep into the mud to swoop the fish into a three-foot net. Both men walk up the bank to a level spot where they whack their fish with a wooden club. After one last shiver, it stops moving.

Upstream where the river is more shallow, anglers stand shoulder-to-shoulder on both sides of the water. There is some poetry in this crowdedness: the fishermen must cast in unison or foul each other's lines. The system is simple. When the bait or lure (here some of the fishermen are using lures and flies) reaches the end of the sweep, the fishermen raise their rods while pulling in the line. The rods are then flipped upstream in a loop, causing the bait to go upstream as well. There the bait hits the water and drops quickly to the bottom.

The fishermen do not seem to be catching fish in this part of the stream, so I move on. Further upstream, just before Ship Creek enters a hatchery, there are crowds milling around a bridge. I learn that the First Annual Ship Creek Salmon Derby is in progress and that prizes are being awarded for the biggest fish. I am tempted to assemble my rod and enter the event, but when I look at my watch, I see that it is almost midnight—and I have to work early tomorrow. It will remain light almost all night long. This midsummer Alaskan light is invigorating and intoxicating. My brain is enchanted and fooled by it. My body needs rest, but I know it will be difficult to sleep. I would almost go to Alaska or other northern climes just to experience this summer light.

After my business in Anchorage is completed, I rent a car and begin driving down the Kenai Peninsula to Soldotna, 150 miles away. At six a.m. the next morning, I am scheduled to meet Bo of Bo's Guide Service. On his brochure Bo is shown holding up a fish that stretches from his mid-thigh to his forehead.

For the first fifty miles en route to Soldotna, the Seward Highway passes along the Turnagain Arm of the Cook Inlet. The road runs right along the foot of the Chugach Mountains where they meet the ocean. The MilePost Travel Guide provides the following warning:

> When the tide is out, the sand in Turnagain Arm might look inviting. DO NOT go out on it. Some of it is quicksand. You could become trapped in the mud and not be rescued before the tide comes in, as happened to a victim in 1989.

Aside from the quicksand, other dangers threaten. On Good Friday of 1964, an earthquake at Portage at the end of Turnagain Arm caused the land to drop twelve feet. Tidal waves swept over the town, wiping out most of the remaining buildings. Then there are the ever-so-slow threats: the glaciers—Skookum, Twentymile and others—grinding their way toward the bay. In 1912 the peninsula was covered with ash when the Katmai volcano erupted. In the short time humankind has been in this area, however, people have managed to do much more damage than the earthquakes or volcanoes. In 1989 the *Exxon Valdez* dumped 250 thousand barrels of crude oil into the fertile waters of Prince William Sound, twenty miles away over the Portage Glacial Road on the Alaska Railroad Shuttle, resulting in the greatest environmental devastation in the history of commercial shipping.

I have other things on my mind than oil spills, however, as I drive on past the train building, such as trying to get a little sleep before I get up to go fishing the next morning. I arrive in Soldotna on the east coast of the Kenai Peninsula at 11:00 at night—dog-tired and very anxious to meet Bo at 5:45 a.m. ("Don't be late," he warned me.)

This is king salmon country. In May and June six to eight hundred thousand king salmon, weighing thirty to forty pounds each, surge up the Kenai River. They are followed by hundreds of thousands of forty to fifty pound kings. These numbers may seem inexhaustible, but equal numbers came up the Sacramento 100 years ago. These fish runs could easily be wiped out by overharvesting.

Five of us settle into Bo's twenty-foot outboard: Bo, his assistant Frank, and a couple from Martinez, California, Shirley and Bob. Shirley and Bob fished with Bo yesterday, landed several big salmon, and are ready to try again. They are both very young, jolly and enthusiastic.

We motor downstream a mile or so and Frank puts globs of fresh-frozen salmon roe on our hooks. The hooks are heavily weighted and designed to drop down to the bottom, where they bounce along in front of the up-coming fish. We have been fishing not more than five minutes when the tip of Shirley's rod dips straight down. When she raises her rod, she discovers she has a

big fish on. Bob jumps up with their camcorder to film the action. Frank and I reel in our lines to get out of Shirley's way.

I am still a little hazy about what actually happened next. Shirley, who could do a weight lifter proud, reels in the line at Herculean speed until the fish can be seen beneath the surface of the water. When the fish reaches us, it leaps out of the river— and right into the boat. The five of us are as surprised to see this forty-five-pound king thrashing around at our feet as he is to see us. There is a stunned pause as all of us stare with our mouths wide open until Frank grabs a wooden club and kills the fish. Shaking and laughing and shouting, Bob says that he might make America's Funniest Home Videos. We wait expectantly while he rewinds the camera. Unfortunately, all he got was the back of our heads, some glimpses of the blue sky, the dark green water, a big fish's tail and some cries of joy and laughter.

To be honest, I am a little confused. The whole sequence seemed so natural, I assumed that these big fish always got reeled in that easily. When Bob hooks the next fish about half an hour later, however, it takes about fifteen to twenty minutes to bring it in. Typically, these fish make great runs away from the boat as soon as they come near it.

I bait up again, but Shirley stops fishing. I ask her if she wants to help me catch my fish. "You can only catch one fish a day," she says. This policy makes it readily clear who has caught a fish that day. By seven o'clock half of the fishermen and women have caught their fish and stopped.

Bo makes several runs through promising holes and then moves on downstream. He has a sonar fish finder to let him know where the fish are, although the flotilla of boats congregating around various places is usually a good enough indication.

By eight o'clock some of the boats have caught their fish and are on their way out.

Bo says, "Come on Barr."

I'm not sure what I am supposed to do now, but I do start to feel a little conspicuous. I wonder if I am missing bites. All of my energy is concentrated on the tip of my rod.

About nine o'clock Frank gets his fish.

Everyone has been successful except me. I sit there, waiting for my fish, while they talk in a jolly fashion. How jolly will they be three hours from now when we are scheduled to quit if I am still keeping them on the river? What if I get a fish on and lose it, or what if I am missing strikes? I had hoped to leave these types of obsessive thoughts at the office.

I begin to strike at everything, which often causes the roe to come off.

Bo says good-naturedly, "Come on Barr."

In response I mumble that we can go in for all I care.

Bob says, "No way, man, get your fish. We like this."

They really don't seem to mind. In fact, they seem content to merely sit in the boat, think about their fish and drift down the river chatting amicably. The river is hypnotic and peaceful. After a while I perceive a rhythm to our movements—the boat drifts down through the hole, the roe hits the bottom, little tug, little tug, little tug. The rod tip dips up and down, up and down, and the boat rocks back and forth, back and forth in the cold, clear water. Then a great bald eagle floats by overhead. I am always elated when I see these majestic birds. They seem to indicate that we are doing something right.

But don't let me get carried away—there is also the roar of boats going up and down the river. The rocking can get violent in the wake of a big boat. The shoreline is not as pretty as it once was. Now it is almost entirely boxed in with little cabins, trailers, docks and discarded junk.

At the mouth of a sidestream, Bo tells me to look at the sonar. It indicates massive numbers of sockeye moving upstream.

Bo hasn't given up. He is working very hard to help me get my fish. He wants me to catch one, not only because then we can all go in and get a cup of cappuccino and he can do repairs on his roof, but because he really wants me to have the experience of catching one. I can see it in his eyes. This is the kind of guide you want—not someone impatient or impulsive, but not someone who will make you feel too entirely at ease either. Bo wants me to feel the pressure. It is the bottom of the ninth, and we are down by three runs. The bases are loaded, there are two outs and two strikes, and only a home run will do.

I never get the home run. I strike out. At noon Bo calls the game.

I sit forlornly on the shore. I wanted so badly to get one of those big fish, and I don't have time for another shift. There is another fishing adventure I want to try—one a little closer to my heart. I have heard that the Russian River sockeye run is on. Sockeye take flies and you can fish directly to them.

I drive back up the Sterling Highway to the place where the Russian River enters the Kenai. When I arrive, the sockeye run is well underway—and what a run it is! The river is thick with these beautiful fish, and the run is now open to the public since enough fish have moved upstream to spawn.

I told some friends in Anchorage that I was planning to fish this river, and they had warned me that it was crowded. I had no idea what crowded could mean in Alaska. This is like fishing on a subway during rush hour.

First, I wait about half an hour before I can even park in the lot serving the Russian River ferry. Then I wait in line to buy a ticket to the ferry. I will have to wait in line still longer before the ferry arrives, then I'll have to get into line again at the other end, just to be able to fish.

Yet the mood is festive, like a tailgate party for a Forty-niner's game. I meet a couple named Frank and Janelle who have emigrated to Alaska from the San Francisco Bay Area. They tell me how happy they are to be here. I ask Frank about flies and show him some of the expensive ones I bought in Anchorage. He says that everybody here uses coho flies, thirty cents apiece, and hands me a package. I feel my little venture is off to a good start.

The Russian River drains the huge glaciated region in the Kenai Fjords National Park. The waters pass through the upper and lower Russian Lakes where the sockeye spawn.

The Russian River ferry is certainly worth the four-dollar fee. The boat is square, seating thirty to forty people. When we are all aboard, the ferryperson releases the boat and the current pulls it downstream while the cable guides it toward the other side. The boat's momentum seems to carry it past the mid-point of the river and then up to the dock on the other side. No motor, no engine, no pollution. I want to discuss the ferry's mechanism with its operator, but I am crushed among the fisher people. We look like a platoon of marines, our fishing rods substituting for guns.

I march up the stream looking for a place to begin fishing. People are spaced every three or four feet as far as I can see up and down the river. Everyone is fishing just a few feet in front of him or her, where the current comes up against the bank. Tasting the waters of their mother stream as it mingles with the Kenai, the fish smell home on this side of the river and hang next to this bank. They are called "reds" because they look bright red in the water.

The fishing rhythm is much the same as the one I had seen on Ship Creek—everyone moving together. The fly or lure is cast upstream as soon as it reaches the end of the run. I assume that many of these people have been here all day.

I finally find a place at the top of the line a mile or more from the ferry. Any fish who makes it up this far has to be some kind of fish. It will have to resist hundreds of coho flies and lures whizzing by in front of it.

A school of sockeye soon approaches. I know they are coming by the intensified splashes of the fishermen's casts. The fish turn back before they quite reach me, but I can see brightly colored flies hanging from the mouths of some. A deep hole is formed where the Russian enters the Kenai about two hundred feet down from me, too deep to wade. I assume that a number of fish wait there until they decide to move up the stream. The intense splashing of the lures seems to confuse the fish and drive them back. Maybe this is why there are not more fish going upstream. They are like captives, beat back by the casting. I feel a little sorry for them, an emotion I try to suppress since I am here to catch them.

What if I get one? I notice that I am using much lighter tackle than most of my shoulder-mates. These are big, strong fish, and they will probably make a pretty big run downstream. I might have to follow the fish, which would mean that I would have to step forward into slightly deeper water and walk downstream, hoping that the other fishermen would lift their rods until the sockeye tired and I could drag it to the shore. It is not long before I have the chance to try all of this out. A big fish grabs my coho fly and starts racing downstream. It is even stronger than I imagined. I hold a tight line, trying to turn the sockeye, not wanting to move too far downstream; yet the fishermen are quite pleasant and don't seem to mind at all as I walk my fish down. Unfortunately, by keeping a tight line and trying to pull in each fish I hook as fast as possible, I lose most of them, banking only one.

This is a diverse fishing group: Inuit, African-Americans, Japanese-Americans, and plenty of others.

An Inuit fishes next to me. He seems bothered by the trouble the fish are having getting up the stream. Like almost everyone I meet, he is from Anchorage. He works in a store and comes down for the "scene."

Toward supper time, the onlookers begin to prepare bankside meals, some on portable stoves, some from richly supplied ice chests. The fish are apparently being saved for later feasts. Except for the Inuit and me, everyone else is fishing for food. They want their two fish, and they are happy when we give them ours.

Most fly fishermen would look contemptuously at this kind of mass fishing, but I find it exhilarating. Had I previously seen a photo of this shoulder-to-shoulder fishing, I would probably never have come here; but I know I am on a great sockeye stream. It is perhaps one of the best in the world. It is within driving distance of Anchorage, and I am here on one of the few days it will be open. I am happy that a few thousand people can get a few meals from this stream—a few special meals. I also like it that all of us can fish together in harmony. There are no harsh words spoken all afternoon and evening, although there are plenty of chances for conflict. We frequently hook each other's tackle, and sometimes we hook each other. Sometimes we don't

Fresh Salmon roasted over a fire is
delicious. I usually lightly coat the
salmon with oil, margarine (or butter)
herbs and spices, as in the following
recipe:

GRILLED SALMON
WITH CILANTRO BUTTER

For the Cilantro Butter:

1/4 cup (2 oz) unsalted butter

3 tablespoons chopped fresh
cilantro

1 1/2 tablespoons fresh lemon or
lime juice

1/4 teaspoon salt

pinch of freshly ground pepper

For the Fish:

2 salmon steaks or skinless fillets
about 1 inch thick

vegetable oil

salt

freshly ground pepper

R. Valentine Atkinson

Position an oiled grill rack 4–6 inches above the fire. To make the cilantro butter, combine the ingredients and melt slowly in saucepan on edge of grill. Sprinkle the fish to taste with salt and pepper. Arrange the fish on the rack. Brush lightly with the melted cilantro butter. Grill 5 minutes then turn and grill for about another 5 minutes. Brush with additional butter and top with slices of lemon and tomatoes. (Lemon and tomatoes can be browned quickly on grill if desired.) The fish is done when it has turned from translucent to opaque throughout.

Nothing can match the enthusiasm generated by the great salmon migration. Elbow-to-elbow and fin-to-fin both human and fish crowd the river in the heat of the excitement. The camaraderie and sportsmanship still prevail, in spite of it all.

Nancy Simmerman

get out of the way in time and cause others to lose a fish. When we bring a sockeye to the bank, however, there is always someone to lend a hand (or net) and offer congratulations. I might break some unspoken rule about the type of tackle needed or how to play a fish, but such indiscretions are politely tolerated. Besides, if the people and the crowding get to us, we can always cast our eyes upward toward the mountains and soar with the eagles.

I have found a few crowded places in Alaska but most are quiet and unspoiled. Alaska has over ten thousand miles of salmon streams, many untouched; yet this resource could vanish as quickly as it has in the lower forty-eight states. Much of Alaska is still wilderness, but every tree and river is in potential danger. What we have done to the fish in the great Pacific Coast rivers stands as a sad reminder of how fragile a seemingly inexhaustible resource can be, and how expensive, difficult, and often impossible it is to correct our mistakes. Fortunately, federal legislation has protected good chunks of Alaska. The Alaska National Interest Lands Conservation Act, passed in 1980, created forty-four million acres of new national parks and preserves, doubled the size of the Arctic National Wildlife Refuge, and protected segments of twenty-five Alaskan rivers. The latter remain vulnerable. Already, vast tracts of Alaska are being clear-cut; plans have been proposed to allow gold mining in many streams, off-shore oil exploration continues, the commercial harvests of chinook and coho salmon are enormous, and the human population grows. The fish must be protected from birth to return to ensure the survival of wild species.

Two hundred miles below the Kenai Peninsula, lies Afognak Island—just north of Kodiak Island, famous for its plentiful brown bears. Afognak is a sparsely inhabited island, covered with old-growth forests where thousands of Sitka black-tailed deer and Roosevelt elk wander. Under terms of the Alaska Native Claims Settlement Act, four hundred thousand acres on Afognak were ceded to the Kodiak Island natives, who in turn sold the timber, mostly to Asian markets. John Eliot, of the *National Geographic,* described the results this way:

> *The most visible of many wounds is a series of nearly continuous clear-cuts. These have left many square miles of ugly stubble where an old-growth forest of Sitka spruce had grown, some of it for 250 years.*
>
> *What remains of Afognak's woodlands is breathtakingly wild.*

The same year, Roy and Shannon Randall, who run the Afognak Wilderness Lodge at Seal Bay, could hear the sounds of a sixteen-member, clear-cutting chain saw team moving close to their idyllic setting. Their wilderness was saved by an ironic twist of fate: Money from a trust fund established from penalties levied against the Exxon Corporation after the *Exxon Valdez* oil spill was used to buy forty-two thousand Afognak acres, including ones close to the lodge. I called Shannon to see what it was like on a March afternoon in the wilderness in Alaska. From the lodge she could see the bay, snow falling gently in the tall trees, and she could hear birds. Referring to the loggers, Shannon said, "Many of the guys were sick to their stomachs to be cutting these trees. Yesterday, I talked to one of them who is now over at Chiniak (on Kodiak Island) where they are doing selective logging. He says it is much better, as both loggers and residents are pleased." It is more expensive to take one tree here and another there, but the forest retains its dignity, and the fish and rivers benefit.

The Salmon People

IN MARCH OF 1778 CAPTAIN JAMES COOK ARRIVED at Nootka Island on the west shore of the Vancouver Island Ranges. He was possibly the first European, and certainly the first Englishman, to contact natives in the region. His ship was greeted by a flotilla of canoes rowed by Nuu-Chah-Nulth natives covered with red paint accentuated with strips of black or white and mica chips for glitter. The natives brought gifts for exchange. A drawing by John Webber, official artist for the expedition, shows us how the village looked. Half a dozen or so square buildings constructed from broad hand-hewn cedar planks sat on the shoreline and were surrounded by a deep forest. One of the buildings appears to have a small totem pole in front of it. The contact with the Europeans would eventually lead to the end of a lifestyle that had developed over many thousands of years. This way of life revolved around the seasons and was made prosperous by the abundant salmon.

Had Cook taken more interest in the natives' lifestyle during his month-long stay on the island, he might have observed an important ritual that unfolded when the salmon began to come up the streams. For the Nuu-Chah-Nulth people and other Northwest Coast native groups, the salmon were not mere fish but the Salmon People who lived in a magic village under the sea. Each year, the Salmon People sent their young men and women in fish disguise to meet the human race and to provide food. As all animals did, the salmon had spirits, abilities and feelings. Their bodies supplied humans with food, and they were happy to give up their flesh if the humans would help their spirits return to their magic village.

The first fish of each species who appeared in the river was a scout for the Salmon People. Depending upon the treatment he received, his people would follow him up the river or stay away. The salmon ceremony evolved as a way to treat this first salmon with due respect.

Ironically, according to oral legend handed down from one generation to the next, the natives who first encountered Cook's ship thought it brought Salmon People in the guise of humans.

Another group of natives whose life revolved around the salmon were the Kwagiutl Indians. Their salmon ceremonies, described in detail by the great anthropologist Franz Boas, who spent parts of several years living with the Kwagiutl people at the turn of this century, are similar to those practiced by most of the Northwest tribes. The Kwagiutl lived on the north of Vancouver Island along Queen Charlotte Strait, which separates Vancouver Island from the British Columbia mainland.

When the first fish of each species appeared, the fishermen ran out to the stream. The fish would be caught by trolling baited, wooden hooks attached to long lines made of strands of braided hair or nettle. Each fisherman would catch four fish, saying:

Welcome, friend Swimmer,

we have met again in good health,

Welcome, Supernatural One,

you, Long-Life-Maker,

for you come to set me right again

as is always done by you.

The fisherman clubbed each fish only once while reciting another prayer:

I do not club you twice, for I do not wish

to club to death your souls so that you may go home

to the place where you came from, Supernatural

Ones, you.

The four fish were then taken by the fisherman's wife to their home where they were placed on a new mat of cedar bark strips made especially for the occasion. Each fish was carefully prepared. First the flesh was cut away. Then the backbone was removed, and sticks were placed across the fish to keep it flat. Finally, the salmon was roasted on a fire. The fish was cooked until the eyes blackened, then the family or sometimes the whole village assembled to eat some of it. The elders prayed,

O, friends! thank you that we meet alive.

We have lived until this time when you come this year …

for that is the reason why you came here,

that we may catch you for food.

We know that only your bodies are dead here,

but your souls come to watch over us

when we are going to eat…

Celebrating the salmon's arrival was a major religious event. It depicted the magical power of transformation embodied in one of nature's greatest miracles—the migration of species. Masks and rattles carved in the images of salmon were used in a potlatch where dancers and shamans performed sacred rituals invoking the presence of spiritual guests.

Supernatural creatures in Kwakiutal Indian myth changed themselves into animals or humans. Dancers dramatized this transformation with masks like the one shown here. The head of the mask opens to reveal a sisiutl, a serpent-like creature.

Nancy Simmerman

Glenbow Museum – Calgary, Alberta, Canada. Cat # R180.219 – photo by Anita Dammer

The natives devised many ways of catching fish. Most often they either speared them or wove nets from nettle hemp and bark. Weirs, essentially a picket fence placed across the stream, were perhaps the most effective fishing method. To create the framework they placed a line of stakes, spaced two or three feet apart, across the river. Then they put sections of lattice against the framework to block the salmon's upward migration. This lattice was made by laying one set of sticks perpendicular to another and then tying them together with cedar strips, cherry bark or some other pliable material. Openings along the length of the weir led to fish traps, also made from lattice sections placed against a frame. The fish would bump along the weir until they swam into the trap, where they were easily caught. Weirs were efficient fishing tools. One large trap built by the Nootka Indians on Vancouver Island took in over seven hundred salmon in fifteen minutes.

After the meal, the salmon bones were all saved and carefully thrown back into the stream so that they could reassemble. If any bones were lost, the Salmon People would be deformed or become angry and not return.

These ceremonies convey a basic wisdom, for honoring and respecting these fish ensures that there will be continuous abundance for all time. The fish and natives served one another well for thousands of years. Europeans brought a very different attitude towards nature: all available resources were to be consumed. They gave little thought to the restoration and preservation of the salmon and their habitat until it was often too late.

Life revolved around the seasons. Spring, summer and early fall were devoted to fishing, gathering berries and preparing for winter. Winter was spent repairing the fishing and hunting gear and performing ceremonies.

The winter ceremonies were so important that the natives of some tribes adopted special winter names, dropping their summer ones. It was believed that evil spirits lurked around the village in wintertime, hoping to harm the villagers. Men and women whose spirits had been captured by the evil spirits could only be restored to the tribe by special rituals. Imagine sitting in a great wooden building built at the edge of the deep forest on a river inlet. It is a dark, rainy night and a fire is raging in the middle of the room. The air is filled with smoke and the sound of batons beating on wooden planks. Then a series of dances begins. Some of these are great fun: the Fool Dancer is teased by the Sparrows who smear grease on his great, long nose. Songs, speeches, comic skits, stories and meals are interwoven throughout the evening. The dancers wear colorful masks, neck rings, ceremonial clothing and jewelry, and carry staffs or weapons. Such ceremonies last for most of the winter. Much of the wonderful art of the Northwest natives was related to these events and the mythology behind them.

Toward the end of an abundant year, the chiefs of various villages would hold a potlatch, a Chinook word that means "the giving of a gift." Potlatches were held to announce, celebrate or honor an event of social significance. Gifts were given to all of the guests. The most valuable gifts were given to the most important people present, and many titles and privileges were bestowed. The formalities of the potlatch could be as complicated as a state dinner at the White House. The invited guests were seated by order of importance. Then dances were performed and songs sung, each symbolizing some aspect of the privileges being granted.

The potlatch culminated in the giving away of the Chief's wealth. A large mat was spread on the floor, and a blanket laid on top of it. Blankets, shirts, shawls, money and many other valuable objects were placed there and given away to the guests. When the gifts were all given, the Chief might ask, "Has anyone been forgotten?" If no one responded, he folded up the blanket and offered it to the guests. The Chief who accepted it was obliged to provide next year's potlatch.

After a potlatch, totem poles might be erected by the host's family. The figures on the poles symbolized the family's ancestry and mythology.

Toward the end of the nineteenth century, Canadian and U.S. Government officials in concert with Christian missionaries, outlawed the potlatches. This outlawing was a part of a program "for the improvement and control of the Indians," as the Canadian Superintendent of Indian Affairs put it. It was not until 1951 that potlatches again became legal, but by then the social structure of the village had long been broken.

The outlawing of the potlatches was only one of many ways that Europeans inexorably changed the lifestyle of these people. These Native Americans had came to the Pacific Coast about ten to fifteen thousand years ago and thrived. At their peak, they numbered about one hundred thousand, living mostly in small villages at the mouths of streams surrounded by the rain forests. In addition to the salmon, the natives ate huckleberries, blackberries and salsal berries. They hunted waterfowl, elk and deer; dug clams, caught crabs and boiled seaweed. There is a Puyallup saying that when the tide is out, the table is set. They built their massive smoke houses and other structures by cutting huge planks from fallen trees using nothing more technologically advanced than stone wedges.

Spaniards were the first Europeans to settle in this area. In 1769 they established a fort on the Olympic Peninsula but gave it up in less than three months, overcome by the constant rain and wild weather. In 1775 seven sailors from the Spanish ship *Sonora* came seeking fresh water from the Olympic Rain Forest and were killed by a party of Quinault Indians.

Lewis and Clark paved the way for white settlement by an overland route. In the late summer of 1805, they crossed over the Continental Divide at Lemhi Pass near Prairie Creek, Montana, and arrived at "a handsome bold runing Creek of cold Clear water." Lewis declared, "here I first tasted the water of the great Columbia river."

Following a trail, they continued into the valley, where the next day they encountered two native women, a man and some dogs who fled as they approached. Soon sixty Shoshone warriors rode up at full gallop. Lewis quickly gave his gun to the other men and, carrying only a flag, strode forward to meet the natives. Seeing that these newcomers meant them no harm, the warriors caressed Lewis and his men and rubbed them with grease from their faces. When Lewis offered them a peace pipe, the natives accepted it and removed their moccasins as an act of friendship, signifying that the white men could traverse their lands. Lewis and his men had not eaten for twenty-four hours. Learning this, the natives provided them with dried cakes of choke cherries and serviceberries, antelope and a piece of salmon. Lewis wrote:

This was the first salmon I had seen, and perfectly convinced me that we were on the waters of the Pacific Ocean.

Later he was served a salmon meal by the Shoshone Indians:

I was furnished with a mat to set on, and one man set about preparing me something to eat, first he brought in a piece of a Drift log of pine and with a wedge of the elks horn, and a malet of Stone curioesly carved he Split the log into Small pieces and lay'd it open on the fire on which he put round Stones, a woman handed him a basket of water and a large Salmon about half Dried, when the Stones were hot he put them into the basket of water with the fish which was soon sufficiently boiled for use it was then taken out put on a platter of rushes neetly made, and set before me ...after eateing the boiled fish which was delicious, I set out.

Contact with the white men would prove disastrous for the natives. By the mid-nineteenth century, ninety percent of the natives had died from smallpox, measles and other European diseases they had no natural immunities against. Those who remained were soon persuaded to sell their lands to the federal government and move onto reservations. Isaac Stevens, the first territorial governor of Washington State, described by his own secretary as a "tiny, bandy-legged tyrant," convinced 171 thousand natives to give up sixty-four million acres for a cost of 1.2 million dollars. The Nez Percé made the best bargain and retained a ten thousand-square-mile reservation on the Snake River and Wallowa Valley. When gold was discovered in the Wallowa Valley, however, miners and homesteaders forced the Indians to give up ninety percent of the reservation. Chief Joseph of the Nez Percé , refused to leave and began a series of skirmishes against the occupying soldiers. The chief and the remnants of his tribe were chased to the Canadian border where they surrendered in 1877. Years later a dam built at Bridgeport, Washington, on the Columbia River was named after him. Ironically, the dam was built without fish ladders, thus killing off whatever remaining salmon had reached that part of the upper Columbia.

By this time in California, silt and run-off from gold mines had begun to ruin the natural color of rivers and kill the salmon. In 1860 the Chimariko Indians began to attack the miners on the Trinity River in Northern California. The miners retaliated. A historian, Stephen Powers, wrote in 1877:

> *(The Chimariko) were hunted to death, shot down one by one, massacred in groups, driven over precipices. …In the summer of 1871 …there was not an Indian left. The gold was gone too, and the miners for the greater part, and amid the stupendous ripping-up and wreck of the earth which miners leave behind them, in this grim and rock-bound canyon …one finds himself indulging in this reflection: "The gold is gone, to return no more: the white man wanted nothing else: the Trinity now has nothing but its salmon to offer; the Indian wanted nothing else."*

Now the salmon are mostly gone too.

Some of the tribes have regained their traditional fishing sites, but only after great controversy. In 1964 the Puyallups in Puget Sound insisted on fishing in the traditional way outside of the regular season. They fished at night but were often caught and jailed. Tension ran high between the white fishermen and the natives. In 1967 a federal judge declared that descendants of the natives in Puget Sound who had signed the original 1854 treaties with Stevens were entitled to half the salmon caught in Washington waters.

Had we retained the reverence held by the Native Americans for the cycles of the fish and the seasons, and for the interconnectedness of our lives with our planet, the wild steelhead and salmon would be in much less danger. The next time I catch one of the Swimmers, I will bless it with a prayer.

I have an even more radical idea. When I die, I would like my ashes cast into the water at the head of some stream. I have not yet chosen one, but there are many candidates: East Mill Creek, the stream of my youth—a quiet brook, that flowed along our front lawn under the cottonwood and sycamore trees; the Smith and Moorehouse in the Unita Mountains where my family had a cabin, and I learned how to fish with lures; the trout streams I love—Henry's Fork, the Green River, the Madison and the Missouri; secret streams of hidden pleasures that must remain unnamed; little streams that need hope and love, like San Francisquito Creek; the salmon and steelhead streams of my middle age; or perhaps the Smith in Northern California, the most beautiful of all and still running freely to the ocean. There are streams in my future that I have yet to explore, and I am not yet ready to decide on my final destination.

King (chinook)

Chum (dog)

Coho (silver)

Sockeye (red)

THE ILLUSTRATED SALMON

The five species of salmon and steelhead undergo physical changes on their upstream journey. In the sea, king, pink, chum, sockeye, and silver salmon and steelheads look very much alike—sleek and silvery. When they enter the streams, however they begin a rapid transformation, driven by a surge of hormones. They change colors, turning reddish, and the males develop a formidable hooked snout. The pink (a peculiar name since they remain green for much of their upstream journey) develop a prominent hump, hence their other name, "humpback." The silver, also called coho, gain a reddish glow. The chum develop vertical red and brown stripes, as though paint were dripped down their sides. Doglike teeth protrude from their overgrown jaws. The sockeye and chinook turn bright red. The steelhead remain least changed, perhaps because, unlike the other Pacific salmon, they return to sea after mating while the others die. On spawning, the steelhead's relationship to the rainbow trout can be seen in the prominent red strip that emerges on its side. These changes serve the fish in their mating rites, but they also make them more visible to predators. Once they enter the stream, the salmon stop eating and have one goal in mind—to return to the site of their origin and mate. The upstream journey, the competition and the spawning take their toll on the fish. Their bottom fins wear away and pieces of skin hang from their thin, tired bodies. Soon their flesh and bones will nourish the stream that gave them life.

Pink (humpback)

Steelhead

RESOURCES

Some of the national and regional organizations involved with conservation and restoration of steelhead and salmon runs and habitats are listed below. This list is by no means exhaustive. In your area there are likely to be groups involved with preserving your local streams.

American Fisheries Society, *5410 Grosvenor Lane, Suite 110, Bethesda, MD 20814-2199*

Association of Northwest Steelheaders, *P.O. Box, 22065 Milwaukee, OR 97222*

California Trout, *870 Market St. #857, San Francisco, CA 94102*

GreenPeace USA, *1436 U Street, NW Washington, DC 20009*

Kenai River Sportfishing Inc., *P.O. Box 1228, Soldotna, AK 99669*

The Nature Conservancy *Pacific Northwest and California offices:*

    Alaska Field Office, 6701 W. 5th, Suite 550, Anchorage, AK 99501, (907) 276-3133

    California Regional Office, 785 Market Street, 3rd Floor, San Francisco, CA 94103, (415) 777-0487

    Oregon Field Office, 1205 NW 25th Avenue, Portland, OR 97210, (503) 228-9561

    Washington Field Office, 217 Pine Street, Suite 1100, Seattle, WA 98101, (206) 343-4344

Oregon Trout, *5331 SW Macadam, Suite 228, Portland, OR 97201*

Portland Audubon Society, *5151 NW Cornell Road, Portland, OR 97210*

Sierra Club, *730 Polk Street, San Francisco, CA 94109*

The Steelhead Society, *P.O. Box 33947, Station D, Vancouver, BC V6J 4L7*

Trout Unlimited, *14101 Parke Long Court, Chantilly, VA 22021-1645, (703) 284-9421*

Washington State Department of Fisheries, Volunteer Fisheries Resource Program, *Room 115, General Administration Building, Olympia, WA 98504-9988*

Washington Trout, *P.O. Box 402, Duvall, WA 98019*

The Wilderness Society, *Pacific Northwest and California Offices:*

    California, 116 New Montgomery Street, Room 526, San Francisco, CA 94105-3607

    Oregon, 610 SW Adler, Suite 915, Portland, OR 97205-3610

    Washington, 1424 Fourth Avenue, Room 816, Seattle, WA 98101-2217

SELECTED BIBLIOGRAPHY

Alkire, C. *The Living Landscape.* Volume 1. Wild salmon as natural capital: Accounting for sustainable use The Wilderness Society, Washington, 1993.

Boas, F., Codere, H. *Kwakiutl Ethnography.* Chicago: The University of Chicago Press, 1966.

Calabi, S. *Trout and Salmon of the World.* Secaucus NJ: Wellfleet Press, 1990.

Campbell, T. Net losses. *Sierra, 76(2),* 48, 1991.

Can we save the Northwest's salmon? Nine leading experts offer solutions. *Trout, 34(3),* 12, 1993.

Connelly, J. The big cut. *Sierra, 76(3),* 42, 1991.

Daniel, J. Dance of denial. *Sierra, 78(2),* 64, 1993.

Deloria, V. *Indians of the Pacific Northwest.* Garden City, NY: Doubleday & Co., 1977.

Eliot, J.L. Kodiak: Alaska's island refuge. *National Geographic, 184(5),* 35, 1993.

Geiger, H.J., Simpson, E. (eds). Preliminary run forecasts and harvest projections for 1994 Alaska salmon fisheries and review of the 1993 season. Alaska Department of Fish and Game. Juneau, AK, 1994.

Hasler, A.D., Sholtz, A.T. *Olfactory Imprinting and Homing in Salmon.* New York: Springer-Verlag, 1983.

Kirk, R. *Tradition and Change on the Northwest Coast.* Seattle, WA: University of Washington Press, 1986.

Lufkin, A. (ed). *California's Salmon and Steelhead.* Berkeley, CA: University of California Press, 1990.

Martin, G. *River: A Reporter's Journey.* San Francisco Chronicle, Special Series Reprint, 1993.

Meyers, S.J. *Streamside Reflections.* San Diego, CA: Thunder Bay Press, 1990.

Northwest Power Planning Council. *Strategy for Salmon.* Volume 2, 1992.

Orr, C.D. Paradise lost. *Wild Steelhead and Atlantic Salmon, 1,* 6, 1994.

Pacific Salmon and Federal Lands: A Regional Analysis. The Wilderness Society, 1993.

Proposal for a study of the status of British Columbia anadromous salmon stocks. Report for Endangered Species Committee, Aquatic Resources Limited, Vancouver, BC, May 1993.

Review of 1993 Ocean Salmon Fisheries. Pacific Fishery Management Council, Portland, Oregon, 1994.

Scott, D. The fight to save Alaska. *Sierra, 76(2),* 40, 1991.

Snake River Salmon Recovery Team: Final Recommendations to the National Marine Fisheries Service. National Marine Fisheries Service, Portland, Oregon, May, 1994.

Stewart, H. *Indian Fishing.* Seattle, WA: University of Washington Press, 1977.

Taylor, D.S. Why wild fish matter: An angler's view. *Trout, 33(3),* 60, 1992.

Van Dyk, J. Long journey of the pacific salmon. *National Geographic, 178(7),* 2, 1990.

White, R.J. Why wild fish matter: A biologist's view. *Trout, 33(3),* 25, 1992.

The Wilderness Society. *The Living Landscape.* Volume 2. Pacific Salmon and Federal Lands: A regional analysis. The Wilderness Society, Washington, 1993.

Williams, T. Alaska plunders its real wealth–undefiled rivers–for a hint of gold. *Audubon, 95(6),* 50,1993.

PERMISSIONS

Egan, T. *The Good Rain.* New York: Vintage, 1991.

Haig-Brown, R.L. Reprinted from *A River Never Sleeps.* by arrangement with the publisher, Lyons & Burford, New York, New York, 1983.

Steinbeck, J. *East of Edan.* (c) renewed 1980 by Elaine Steinbeck, John Steinbeck IV, Thom Steinbeck. Used by permission of Viking Penguin, a division of Penguin Books, USA Inc.